Tagore and Social Work

About the Authors

Dr. Joëlle Libois has a doctorate in educational sciences and since 2011 has been Director of the School of Social Work (HES-SO) in Geneva. She received initial training in social work and also specialized in clinical approach to social work. Her professional experience in the fields of social education and community development has led her to focus on relational and affective dimensions, and the notion of presence which is the foundation of social work. Passionate about India for over thirty years, she has developed educational and sustainable development projects in several states of India, and has a major interest in the thought and works of Rabindranath Tagore. Today, a partnership has been established between the Social Work Department of Visva-Bharati University and the Higher School of Social Work in Geneva, Switzerland.

Kumkum Bhattacharya, Professor, Department of Social Work, Visva-Bharati has been teaching since 1979. She has wide experience of research among tribes of eastern India, especially the Santals and other minority communities. One of her areas of interest is culture-personality studies and the various ways in which minorities and marginalized communities constitute the plurality of Indian civilization. She is also interested in understanding the ways in which minorities and marginalized communities adjust and adapt to plural situations. The other abiding area of academic interest is revisiting Tagore's ideas of Rural Reconstruction and the role of a university in extension activities. She has recently published *Rabindranath Tagore: Adventure of Ideas and Innovative Practices in Education,* Springer International (2014). She may be contacted at kmkm.bh@gmail.com and her profile may be accessed www.visva-bharati.ac.in

Dr. Prasanta Kumar Ghosh is currently a Professor in the Department of Social Work, Visva-Bharati University. He has served the Department of PM & IR, Tata Institute of Social Sciences, Mumbai as a Reader and Principal of the Institute of Rural Reconstruction, Visva-Bharati. He published books and articles in journals at national and international levels. He is a proactive social work educator, researcher and activist.

He is a Fulbright Fellow, USIEF, on Academic Administration. He has also served as Visiting Professor at the University of Illinois, Urbana, Dominican University, Chicago, USA and School of Social Work, University of West Switzerland, Geneva. Apart from teaching and research he is engaged in community development by organizing rural entrepreneurs through social entrepreneurship organizations since last 30 years to fight against poverty encountered by the rural poor.

Tagore and Social Work

A Universal Inspiration

Joëlle Libois
Kumkum Bhattacharya
Prasanta Kumar Ghosh

CONCEPT PUBLISHING COMPANY PVT. LTD.
NEW DELHI-110059

ISBN-13: 978-93-5439-087-6

First Published 2022

Published and Printed by

Concept Since 1974

Concept Publishing Company Pvt. Ltd.
A/15-16, Commercial Block, Mohan Garden,
New Delhi-110059 (India)
T: 91 11 41101460
E: publishing@conceptpub.com, *W*: www.conceptpub.com

Cataloging in Publication Data--Courtesy: D.K. Agencies (P) Ltd. <docinfo@dkagencies.com>

Libois, Joëlle, author.

Tagore and social work : a universal inspiration / Joëlle Libois, Kumkum Bhattacharya, Prasanta Kumar Ghosh.

pages cm

Includes bibliographical references and index.

ISBN 9789354390876

1. Tagore, Rabindranath, 1861-1941--Political and social views. 2. Social service--India. I. Bhattacharya, Kumkum, 1955- author. II. Ghosh, Prasanta Kumar (Professor of social work), author. III. Title.

LCC HV393.L53 2022 | DDC 361.954 23

Acknowledgements

The authors would like to put on record their individual and collective gratitude to the many persons who have partnered, helped and encouraged in the making of this book. Magdalena Chrusciel helped in translating from the French to English and in the interpretation of the deep meanings of the writings of Tagore; Mira Ghosh, a specialist in the songs of Tagore and a friend of many years in Santinketan who was responsible in the initial introduction of the authors with each other; Frances Salmon for her willingness to be on hand with the proof reading and suggestions and Rene Schindler who encouraged in this great writing adventure with the colleagues and friends. We are grateful to the Director, HESSO, Geneva for supporting the MOU between the two institutions, HES-SO and Visva-Bharati University.

We also take this opportunity to thank Sherry Joseph for allowing us to share in his work (joint); Fakrul Alam for translating the poems and songs used in this book; Sreya Mitra for her assistance in reference work and Samit Dasgupta who helped in the page lay-out and computer input.

The authors express their sincere thanks to the Visva-Bharati and the School of Social Work, Geneva for their support.

Contents

1

Introduction

'...our problem is world-wide and no one people of the earth can work out its salvation by detaching itself from others. Either we be saved together or drawn together into destruction'.[1]

I. Introducing the Backdrop of the Volume

Human problems are universal and universal are the services that people need wherever they may be. The more civilized or advanced we become, nations, communities, groups or individuals; none can afford to look at problems and situations in isolation from world events and conditions as the solutions perforce rest on collective endeavour and in joining of forces. The more we are able to think of the world as a 'global village' the more sustaining will be our efforts at creating an enabled people and world. It is against this backdrop that the ideas of Tagore come to the fore that make us once again believe in the poet's words quoted above. These words written almost a hundred years ago had sprung in response to the strife of that part of our history but are as relevant in our contemporary times. Tagore seemed to have realized the importance about universal human connections. His great faith in humanity as a whole; his nuanced understanding of nation and patriotism; and that the purpose of human existence vested in creative extension of the individual self to the community for shared growth and development need to be highlighted as another viable alternative that the newer generations can explore and work on. The book aims to acknowledge Tagore's pioneering ideas and put a human face to what are understood as facets of development.

The authors from two parts of the globe, Switzerland and India teaching and practicing Social Work as a profession and discipline bring their long years of experience and thoughts to coalesce in this volume; those that are organically linked to the ideas Tagore gave shape to when he founded his university in 1922. There is a certain paucity of material on Tagore's hands-on work in the villages of Bengal as a precursor of what would later emerge as a discipline for students to study and become professional social workers. In fact, in talking of Tagore's work initiated as far back as 1922 with the help and partnership of L.K. Elmhirst, a British agricultural scientist, it is difficult to find reference material and the fact that much of the available material is dated. Contemporary discourse on the innovative Sriniketan Experiment is absent in academia. In the contemporary time, there has been a quantum leap in interest among students, teachers and researchers for who this volume is a step. Contemporizing Tagore's ideas was the impetus behind this volume with the objective of inspiring students who come to Social Work.

Tagore's ideas were born from the conjunction of his experiences of the villages of Bengal and of the contrasting metropolitan culture of the east and west. Tagore was always conscious that humanity had a lot to gain from exchange and interaction sans borders or ideas of nation/nationality. The authors seek to use this text as a means of engaging the younger generation of Social Workers so that they too feel a sense of solidarity across the world and see humanity in entirety. It is not just an ideology that this book promotes but rather, to demonstrate, that a poet had enough conviction to construct an institution on the basis of that ideology, the core essence being fluid and dynamic. That Tagore was a champion of change and eagerly kept himself abreast of all that was happening around the world is not so much discussed or debated among the contemporary academicians and social workers around the world.

These ideas briefly set the tone and tenor of this volume.

II. Encountering the West

At the young age of 17 years Rabindranath Tagore (1861-1941) travelled to London sailing from Bombay in 1878. This was quite *de rigueur* for the elite in India to travel to England to train for the Bar to become a professional barrister or the practitioner of law. Rabindranath's family was no exception to this practice as his second elder brother, Satyendranath had already qualified for the prestigious Indian Civil Services while Rabindranath appeared to be drifting in his life, happiest among his poetry and books. It is interesting to note that of the fourteen siblings, none other than Rabindranath's brother Satyendranath ever had a job though they each had their special talents with which they remained occupied. Rabindranath was the youngest in the family. Prior to his departure for England Rabindranath spent some months living with an anglicized family in Bombay, the Tarkhade family, to learn the 'arts' of living among the English. He was from his childhood home schooled in all possible subjects ranging from astronomy, physics, chemistry, biology, history, philosophy, music, literature of the world and languages. From a very young age he would be assigned tasks of translation from one language to another and on his own learnt, passably well, to read and translate as exercise, German and other European languages. Piano was an instrument that he was familiar with right from his childhood – the Tagore hereditary home in Calcutta (now Kolkata) was the hub of cultural and social activities and gatherings. It was truly a renaissance home filled with liberal ideas, wide interests and varied ways of encountering culture that transcended not only the city, but also the country (India) and embraced the world.

Even before reaching the shores of England, young Rabindranath was prepared to be enchanted – his attraction stemmed from his broad and wide exposure to European classics in literature, music, philosophy, science and education. He was an exceptionally handsome man, over 6ft. tall, with the look of a budding poet in the style of the romantic poets of England. He was shy in company and quiet; not sure about his skills of interaction and the fact that he was hitherto unaccustomed to what can be called 'small talk' or social conversation. He would readily come into his own when asked to sing his songs accompanied on the piano that he played amateurishly. Rabindranath was exposed to a variety of English and European songs and music in the social gatherings he attended and receptive as he picked up the tunes that he later put to innovative use in his own musical compositions. There were Irish, English, German tunes and airs that he later used with fascinating effect in composing songs in his mother tongue, Bengali. The account of his experiences of this first visit to western shores reach us through the letters he wrote home published on his return in 1880 (*Letters from a Sojourner in Europe*).

These details highlight Tagore's immense capacity to absorb, internalize and profit from new experiences – he questioned, compared, weighed the good and bad and had the ability to adapt without losing his own deep moorings in the tradition and culture to which he belonged. He was deeply moved by English society especially their attitudes towards women, children, civility and the informed taste for culture. Tagore did not see the world split into the binary of east and west – for him humanity was of utmost importance and that there was much that could be learned for the advantage and advancement of all through mutual efforts. Knowledge, he believed could not be bound by geography or creed but attained through continuous and involved creative engagement with life and intellect guided by curiosity and experienced as joy. To express this more clearly, the key elements of Tagore's 'philosophy' centered in the free spread of knowledge and wisdom which according to him was not a one-way traffic from the occident to the orient (or the other way) and knowledge was to be pursued for which he believed that the west had developed institutions, ideologies and trained minds to deal with issues of knowledge generation, innovative thinking and finding solutions in which India was lacking. Education was also not uni-directed of the learned towards the unlettered; rather he believed that there was much to learn from each other if the relationship between the lettered and unlettered was based on fellowship and mutual trust. Many years later a similar idea is found resonating in the works of Paulo Freire

(1970). In fact, as has been iterated in this book, this relationship of fellowship and trust between the lettered and the unlettered forms the bedrock of the experiment of Rural Reconstruction that formally began in 1922 in Visva-Bharati. Education for Tagore was the path to human development through which social growth could be fostered.

III. Why Education?

Rabindranath Tagore spanned almost two halves of two centuries that stood witness to change in India and the world on an unprecedented scale in almost all spheres of life. The awakening of India starts on the one hand, with the discourse on the need to 'cleanse' caste-ridden Indian society, a process initiated by Raja Rammohun Roy (1772-1833) known as the father of Indian Renaissance and on the other, the ushering of modernism with the advent of the British in India. Rammohun Roy exercised a profound influence on the Tagore family starting with Tagore's grandfather, Prince Dwarakanath Tagore, father Debendranath Tagore and Tagore himself. It was primarily the Tagore family who were the carriers and patrons of Roy's ides of social reforms, especially in sustaining and achieving the ideals of the Brahmo Samaj, the religion of a newly awakened India and Roy's educational thoughts found resonance in Tagore's own cogitations and praxis.

Tagore notwithstanding in his own words being '...a poet first and a poet last...'[2] was one of the key figures of the extent as well as in shaping of that change in India; in fact, Tagore is universally acknowledged as one of the key makers of modern India and a significant contributor to the idea of universalism in large parts of the world.[3] He believed that the principal means of effective and sustained change in the conditions of lives of the underprivileged and oppressed would come through education. The structure and pedagogy of education was a great concern of Tagore. He showed interest in education from very early in his life and he had strong conviction that education changed society. Undoubtedly, education allows individuals access to the ocean of knowledge and this sets in motion the channels of communication by which universal aims and objectives are realized through which societies become progressive. Educated individuals learn to question social norms, religious compulsions, economic and political structures.[4] Also, education forms bridges or links between people reducing the divide between the literate and illiterate when the literate are actively motivated to be of service to society at large. Tagore was deeply sensitive to the general fate of the large majority of India's rural population being denied all light of education and progress. With a mass of stagnant rural population only relegated to agriculture related economy no country could ever hope to progress beyond a point. There was and is a need to build educational systems and institutions that are rooted in such values and principles of seeking knowledge; generating new knowledge and using those skills to be in service of those who are not so privileged; he hoped that this would allow greater mass participation sans caste or creed. '...in the present age with its facility of communication...the great federation of men...a unity, wider in range, deeper in sentiment, stronger in power than ever before'[5] can make for true education. It is clear that Tagore did not mean either the prevalent tradition of religious teaching in the country or the British colonial education system in the context of his educational ideals.

IV. The Cross-Currents of New Thinking

How is Rabindranath Tagore or Tagore as he came to be called, placed in the western world? That the western world was emerging as economically powerful and advanced in terms of knowledge was an established fact. 'From the early decades of the nineteenth century, an informed awareness of the west became an overpowering presence in the consciousness of educated Indians. ...There was a fairly universal recognition that the west was now dominant.... An attitude to knowledge, ... was the key factor in the triumph of the west.'[6]

Tagore, all through his life was acutely conscious of the need for an education that would prepare man for the modern world not from a point of view of narrow nationalism but spreading out its wings to embrace the feeling of universalism and global kinship. His words ring true for every professional social worker who has an eye to the distant future embracing the whole of mankind in that single gaze. Education as well as its derivatives is not just building knowledge but in learning to be responsible, self-determined, sensitive to the aspirations, struggles and distress of his countrymen and having the will to resolve the conflicts between the old (tradition) and the new (modernity). During the time when India was under colonial rule and educational systems were increasingly coming under colonial influence and priority Tagore stood tall with his cry, 'I repeat our education is the thing we should first take into our own hands'.[7] Tagore laid great store by his belief that it was self-determination that above all had the capacity to strengthen the nation from below or the grassroots.

Let us take you back to 1930 when Tagore visited Odenwaldschule, the school set up by Paul Geheeb and his wife, Edith. It was remarked that both Tagore and Geheeb brought the offering of love and simple faith to the altar of the God of humanity. Tagore after his visit had written, 'Every child comes with the message that God is not discouraged of man'. Tagore wrote to Geheeb in response to an invitation for Tagore's active participation in the World Conference of the New Education Fellowship, 'Enlightened education and organizations like your Insitut Monnier and my Santiniketan have indeed a great role to play in saving civilization'.[8] The circumstances of world history forced Geheeb to relocate his school along with thirty students from Germany to the Swiss Alps calling it Ecole d'Humanite functioning even today and regarded highly. Switzerland was the one neutral haven sheltering the educationist Geheeb and his troop.[9]

Tagore and his international circle would remain incomplete if there is no mention of Romain Rolland (1866-1944) and his deep friendship with Tagore and admiration for Mahatma Gandhi. It was Rolland who brought to larger notice, Tagore's ideas against narrow nationalism with his letter of appreciation in 1919. Rolland persuaded Tagore to put his signature on the *La Déclaration pour l' indépendence de l'esprit,* which was probably the first organized attempt to mobilize intellectual opinion across the globe against war. The two met in Geneva in 1930.[10]

In 1926, Tagore came in contact with Maria Montessori whose methods he admired and agreed to inaugurate the Benares Montessori School in India. The work of L.K. Elmhirst and his wife, Dorothy Straight at Dartington Hall, Britain, without who a lot of Sriniketan (details of which are available in chapter IV of this book) would not have been possible continued to interest Tagore as he saw in Dartington a continuation of the institutional model that he had himself been trying to build; he considered his work as always being-in-progress. Tagore was greatly influenced by Spencer, Rousseau, Locke and Dewey; he had affinity with the reformist zeal of Pestalozzi and Froebel; he was also very impressed with the holistic vision of society and individual and their interplay shared and propagated by both Patrick Geddes and his son Arthur Geddes. Tagore was aware of Tolstoy's Yasnaya Polyana as well as Thoreau's *Walden*. These were revolutionary thinkers of their time and contemporary to Tagore.[11] Most of the above personalities believed in the idea of freedom and emancipation of the spirit for the complete person to blossom in which education played a pivotal role.

The year was 1918; Tagore wrote to Rathindranath, his son, from Los Angeles, '... the Santiniketan school should form a link between India and the world – there has to be founded the centre for cultivating universal manhood – the epoch of narrow nationalism is coming to its end – the grand ceremony of the great union of the nations of the world shall have its beginnings on the fields of Bolpur. It is my first desire to build that spot as one transcending the barrier of nationalistic geography. The first flag of victory of the Universal Man shall be planted there.'[12] It is interesting to note that Tagore chose the outskirts of a tiny rural township of Bolpur quite a distance away from the bustling city of Calcutta (now Kolkata) for his grand university. Lore has that there were only few palm trees and arid open spaces with almost no vegetation. This was the same place where in 1901, he had started his *asrama*-school (modern hermitage); he visualized the school forming the nucleus of the university – the child going through a process of transformation into a creative being. Tagore thought of a university as fulfilling the role of fostering mutual understanding between the east and west and the opportunity for working together sharing humanity's common intellectual and artistic heritage. In a letter[13] Tagore wrote, 'Visva-Bharati ... will be a pilgrimage. Let those coming to it say, oh what a relief it is to be away from narrow domestic walls and to behold the universe'. We could here aptly recall Tagore's poem from the Gitanjali (1910),

> Where the mind is without fear and the head is held high;
> Where knowledge is free;
> Where the world has not been broken up into narrow fragments by narrow domestic walls;
> Where words come out from the depth of truth;
> Where tireless striving stretches its arms towards perfection;
> Where the clear stream of reason has not lost its way into the dreary desert sand of dead habit;
> Where the mind is led forward to thee into ever-widening thought and action –
> Into that heaven of freedom, my Father, let my country awake.[14]

India had her first modern universities under British rule in 1857; however, they were not teaching universities till about 1920; thus, we have to see Tagore's initiative and endeavour as not only innovative but as radical and of special interest to us as social workers. This is considered as a fundamental step or stage to set in motion empowering and liberating social action and change not within the confines of any one nation but embracing the whole of humanity. I personally think that this has been the guiding principle of western efforts to take social work philosophy, values, principles, perspectives to all those places in the world where there is need and gaps are to be filled. Understanding the aspects of universal human need for social service is the key to comprehend the collective global response that we see from the beginning of the 20th century.[15] Tagore's role in these efforts had indeed been path breaking.

V. Arrival at the Core Areas of Tagore's Thoughts[16]

To further clarify Tagore's emphasis on the relation of education and social work we need to understand the different phases that helped in this process – right in his early manhood (1891) he was sent by his father to manage the family estates in erstwhile East Bengal (now Bangladesh) where he spent almost ten years of his life with his young and growing family. Of course, the first thought in his mind was arranging the education of his children in the 'dark and ignorant' hinterlands of the country but he was also confronted with the besetting problems and conditions of rural life. This first phase is transformative – he articulated his ideas and thoughts presenting them to the outside world through his letters and essays. Tagore was not just talking back to the Raj (referring to the two century British rule in India till its independence in 1947) but starting a movement from which, the world at large could learn. The next phase is the actual formation of the university called Visva-Bharati (1918) with the motto 'Here the world builds its home in a single nest' while the next and final phase could clearly be defined and identified with his work on manifesting his ideas of Rural Reconstruction in Sriniketan, the twin campus of Visva-Bharati established in 1922.[17] Here was the scope for application of knowledge; of extending the self in service to people and training the hitherto uncared for rural mass to become active in their own 'deliverance'. Tagore had remarked, '...by country we mean the country of the gentlefolk alone. The common people we contemptuously describe as the "lower class". This appellation has entered into our marrow since a long time now. ... We belong to the same country, yet we are strangers to one another.[18]

In order to understand and appreciate Tagorean ideas of Social Work it was important for the writers to start with his innovative and path breaking ideas on education because of the tremendous stress he laid on it (education) as the one meaningful path to human development. For Tagore, human development and education were not merely individual endeavours, rather they could be achieved in large measure through collective and symbiotic efforts to which he attributed the work of social work in communities. In this volume, the authors have made an attempt to present a comprehensive picture of Tagore's ideas on community and social work founded on the principles of human development and education.

It is easy to recognize the poverty of physical hunger, of disease, of lack of hygiene, but the poverty of the very spirit of man is not always visible and more, not easy to deal with. The poverty of the spirit robs man of initiative, of agency, of hope to be able to fulfill potential. India for millennia has been a land of villages whose primary production was agriculture and yet it has one of the oldest civilizations of the world. India has been conquered from outside, occupied for long periods of time and yet we do not find a subjugated or colonized people. It is indeed remarkable that so much has survived the ravages of time and history. India has been more interested in the broadcast of her culture and ideas. It had one of the longest freedom struggles in the history of mankind but somehow the tempo of life was not violently disturbed. The disturbance in this rhythm manifested during the colonial rule because of the attitudinal stance of the colonizer who sought to create the home-away-from-home with the 'native' seen as incidental in their newly acquired lands. The emergence and the nurturance of the cities during the British rule with its practices in public education, governance centres, public entertainment etc. eroded the traditional systems in each of the above. The few emerging urban locations became dominant in terms of their influence and attractiveness.

From a largely oral tradition there was a rapid shift to the written tradition that used to be restricted to the very few and literacy became an important benchmark to differentiate between those who could and could not (read and write). Education under colonial rule was closely linked to job opportunity in government sectors with little else besides. These employment opportunities were certainly not white-collar and neither was it in the primary sector, agriculture. Industrialization was bringing in another kind of employment opportunity through skill education and training. Cities or urban centres seemed better equipped to house and service these large public institutions of education and training in economically viable ways. This marked a break in the continuity of life between rural and urban; the urban population did not have much use for the education traditionally followed in the country as it neither provided employment nor did people regard it with the former awe whereas the rural population felt that all modern opportunities were outside their realm of life. This further resulted in a skewed balance in favour of 'modernity' against 'tradition'. This schism (between tradition and modernity) went deep into the psyche of the people.

It was against this backdrop that Rabindranath's rural experiment is better understood and we are able to appreciate the very modern or progressive nuances that he brought into it. He had faith in the strength of tradition leading to modernity; i.e., the continuum of 'tradition-modernity' in which the continuity of knowledge is more seamlessly linked to each other in mutual support and nurturance. He was conscious that modernity had little place for then existing in-built social distinctions or restricting access to knowledge and it was towards this goal that he designed an inclusive system by which the so-called uneducated and the educated could find a common meeting ground both located in tradition while engaging themselves with emerging modernity. This shift from a passive imitator (in response to the aura of modernity and total rejection of tradition) to an active participant (one who is capable of making a critical response to the dominant form of modernity in the light of the strengths of tradition) has always been the hallmark of his experiments in rural reconstruction, the focal area of this volume. It is Tagore's work in Rural Reconstruction that laid the foundation of Social Work taught and practised in Visva-Bharati and in other parts of India attracting scholars and activists from far and wide. His ideas have inspired subsequent social activism, initiatives and social movements.

He had noticed that rural people showed a tendency to shirk from exercising their agency for their own good while at the same time believed in an exaggerated idea of the powers of the city-dwellers; he further observed that traditional cultures were not being replenished while modernity was largely a matter of imitation; rural life was hardly a concern for the state machinery other than sources of revenue; the rural people who received modern education became alienated from their own societies and he also felt that rural societies were not appreciated or recognized for the services they provided without which the very existence of mankind would have been at stake.

The Institute of Rural Reconstruction from its inception was engaged in health, hygiene, youth and children, reproductive health, channeling the creative energies of women and setting up grain banks in the surrounding villages. Rabindranath was pragmatic enough to realize his limitations in terms of finance and the scope of rural work and was very clear that he would work within those limits. For him it was not a case of replication of successful 'cases' (villages) but the lighting of at least a "few lamps" to show evidence that light could emanate from hitherto dark corners.

VI. The Polemics of Reconstruction:

Rabindranath's word, *punargathan* has been unhappily translated as 'reconstruction' but for the want of a more appropriate word we shall assume that *punargathan* and reconstruction indicate the same processes and purposes. We could also explore if Tagore's ideas of reconstruction and concept of development are synonymous especially given our contemporary engagement and faith in the term 'development'. Why did Rabindranath choose the term 'reconstruction' over 'development'? Being the wordsmith that he was, the semantics of the term and more, it is clear why 'reconstruction' won! Even in the face of the inevitability of change, Rabindranath stressed on well-considered change not always from above but emerging from within the people so that change would be suited to the times. This brings the discussion to the term 'tradition' and its meanings; we shall take 'tradition' as being one end of the tradition-modernity continuum. We could in the context of Social Work consider traditional/modern being **attitudinal stances** adopted to confront human conditions of existence/living. Following the latter dimension of distinction, it is posited that rural-urban continuum often hinges on the attitudinal differences in confronting human conditions in the following manner – rural societies tend towards the tradition while urban societies have the scope to pursue modernity and at the same time re-shape tradition. However, this is not to gainsay the fact that tradition has always been the bedrock on which any modernity is built. Reconstruction suggests that there is scope to reinvigorate/revitalize the once pulsating life that has since become moribund. The resource is, as if, dormant waiting for the waking nudge – to be roused from slumber. Slumber takes the form of abnegating responsibility, a withdrawal of individual/collective agency; slumber is dependency and slumber is avoiding reason.

VII. Sriniketan Experiment Today

1921 or the year when Tagore started putting together the practical part of his Rural Reconstruction, the scenario in rural West Bengal and India was virginal – no government programmes of uplift or intervention or even policy were in force or even visible. Tagore's ideas were communicated to the village people by a group of highly dedicated workers at the grassroots level. The message was new, the tasks required participation and the foundation of work rested on mutual respect and exchange; smaller units or villages were the targets and the people were collectively brought under the umbrella of Visva-Bharati University. The tasks of civic nature, providing health services including safe child birth, education, child care and training of women in generating income, forming youth groups who would work as the ears and eyes of Visva-Bharati, training craftspersons in polishing their skills and marketing their products, special attention to improved agricultural practices etc. enfolded every section of the community and impacted practically every life. This inclusive and holistic approach won Tagore the goodwill of the people in large measure who also felt that they had ownership of the changes that were initiated and effected. That the university did not have an unlimited or even adequate fund was clearly understood by the people of the villages thus a feeling of independence among the common people was fostered.

India gained her freedom in 1947; six years after Tagore passed away in 1941. Between 1941 and 1951 (when Visva-Bharati was established as a Central University) Tagore's son Rathindranath valiantly tried to sustain the work of Sriniketan. The Institute of Crafts in Sriniketan was a commercial success with its innovative designs and craftsmanship that was highly reputed. The other departments in Sriniketan had to make do with dwindling workforce as salaries could not be arranged for direct village work. On the other hand, soon after independence rapid urbanization engendered quite different aspirations and needs among people and communities. The government with its intention of attending to the entire population designed plans, schemes, programmes, enacted laws, took measures, created institutions etc. so as to penetrate into the entire country albeit with a diverse population. The role of Sriniketan from being a 'doing agency' changed into a 'learning-teaching agency' and as a result took up the challenge of training the manpower who would be suited for the government's task of nation-building. The government designed its community-based Block Development, discussed in detail in Chapter 3, based on the ideas of Rural Reconstruction adapted to its time-bound framework of development. The villages in and around Sriniketan became 'beneficiaries' and not the 'actors'. Over the years Sriniketan has worked on how to fill in the gaps in inclusive governance and how people can be empowered to stake their own claims through education, awareness, mediation and negotiation for which skill-based training of villagers is included in the domain of Sriniketan Experiment. Now it is no longer an experiment – it is a holistic approach to capacity building, understanding of rights and duties and self-enhancement.[19]

Tagore captured the imagination of the occident in ways very few have done – a variety of reasons can be cited. In the second chapter Tagore's firm belief in universalism, aesthetics, spirituality (sans religion) and his relentless endeavour to give shape to his ideals have been cogently and succinctly presented. The trajectory through which Tagore travelled in his adventure of ideas and his experience of the realities of life in varied and various settings has in this volume been clearly shown. His almost instinctive response to the need for modernity and change tempered by liberal thinking and ideals form the crux of this volume. In the subsequent chapters we find the '*Karma Yogi*' Tagore no longer in his armchair ruminating in the abstract world; rather we find a Tagore who was eager to get his 'hands dirty' with real work with real people. The accounts of the extent Tagore went to give shape to his ideas have been substantiated and documented in this volume. There is still insufficient literature available on the many shades of the Sriniketan Experiment launched by Tagore formally in 1922 with the help of L.K. Elmhirst; the subsequent chapters in the volume fill in those gaps to a great extent. Each chapter in the book dovetails into the other complementing while also raising their individual focus issues.

It has been a privilege to be part of this volume for all of us – the time is just right for the world to have a nuanced and intimate knowledge of the ideas and practices that Tagore stood for. For too long the world has become accustomed to dress Tagore in the garb of a poet and a mystic savior of humanity – he is certainly more than that and there is much that we can gain from knowing him. He was as much a thinker as a doer – he never let himself rest till he had given shape to his ideas to be put to the test to see if they worked. That he had a modern scientific temper is clear – pontification was not his goal. Gandhi likewise, shared in these ways of thinking and doing though using his own means of advancing his ends. The central theme that interlinked their ideas and actions was that human potential is limitless and that human conditions are shared; it is in the action that effective change can be brought. These are the lessons that we wish to impart to students of social work – to be true to reality when engaged in intervention or in need-assessment of human conditions against the backdrop of human potential and commonality of human conditions.

The authors come from the west and east bringing with them years of experience in social work practice and theory in contemporary times – it is significant that they take a fresh look at Tagorean ideas with the view to give their students an orientation to modern ideas of social work that needs rejuvenation of some sort at intervals of time. The time is right for a re-look. The world and its problems do not show signs of abating or even changing conditions fundamentally – there is a continuing cycle of adding to the numbers of the hungry, the ill, the poor, the uneducated, the oppressed and there is also the great need to recognize the supra-organic shape of modern commerce that does not seem to have any core human values or even a human face. It is in the context of this Tagore's interpretation of the conjunction of the 3 P's, a buzzword in corporate social responsibility, could suggest a new direction to Social Work practice – *people* (individual, community), *planet* (earth, environment, its protection and conservation) and *profit* (generating human capital based on education, health and meaningful occupation) that would thus enable people's capabilities of giving back to the social system of their creative energies in service to all. The Social Worker today carries heavy responsibilities but she has to do it with a light and engaged touch; she needs to expand her mental vistas to carry more knowledge and expertise; she needs to accommodate the various lineages of thought available in different cultures and societies so that the experience of engaging in Social Work is both intellectually stimulating and effective in inducing change.

In this volume we have taken two different perspectives in understanding the relationship between Tagore and Social Work. There is focus on Tagore the person; his family background and the genesis of his progressive ideas. Tagore was a major player in the great social revolution that was making its presence felt in the form of the Bengal renaissance working with a host of social reformers. The social history of Bengal and the role of the Tagore family was a significant benchmark of the push to social change at very fundamental levels. It was also the indigenous way of talking back to the colonial rule not really as a contrary force but based on the idea of cooperation and natural partnership of humanity. After creating the backdrop explaining why Tagore engaged himself in social work/service the focus then is on the practical aspects of his work and the principles that he identified as important in social work; principles accepted in contemporary ideas that form the foundation of social work. Long before the rights-based approach and the strengths perspective gained importance in contemporary social work curriculum, Tagore was already dabbling with them while designing his Sriniketan Experiment on Rural Reconstruction. From the chapters on Tagore's principles and philosophy the authors have tried to look at the Cooperative Movement as ideated by him. One of the important chapters is on values that emerge from Tagore's practice-based work involving trial and error, innovation and continuous and persistent efforts.

This slim volume is multi-faceted and multi-voiced from which we hope that the younger generation will have much to take away and internalize in their own understanding and practice of social work. They will learn of the value of the educated extending their selves for those not so fortunate so that there is more equitable justice and harmony in society where disparity can be mitigated to a certain extent.

BIBLIOGRAPHICAL REFERENCES

Anisuzzaman, , 'Ihajagatika', in *Ihajagatika O Ananya,* Kolkata, Karigar. 2012.

Bhattacharya, Kumkum. "Utopias in Praxis: Rabindranath's Rural Reconstruction" in *Utopias from Asia.* edited by Konrad Meisig, Germany, Harrassowitz Verlag. 2012.

-*Adventure of Ideas and Innovative Practices in Education.* Springer International. 2014.

Bhattacharya, Sabyasachi. *Rabindranath Tagore: An Interpretation*, India, Viking Penguin. 2011.

Chakravarty, Amiya (ed.). *Tagore Reader.* "RNT in conversation with Romain Rolland". accessed http://academic.udayton.edu/monishchatterjee/tagore/rolland.html (01.05.2019).

Dasgupta, Uma. *Selected Writings on Education and Nationalism,* New Delhi, Oxford University Press. 2009.

Freire, Paulo. 1970. *The Pedagogy of the Oppressed.* New York. Herder and Herder.

Kaempchen, Martin 2017-18, *Rabindranath Tagore Meets Paul and Edith Geheeb: An Indo-German Encounter* (project submitted to Indian Institute of Advanced Studies, Simla, India.

-2020, *Indo-German Exchanges in Education.* Oxford University Press. New Delhi India.

Mukherjee, H.B. 2013, *Education for Fullness: A Study of the Educational Thoughts and Experiment of Rabindranath Tagore*, India, Routledge, pp.419-420

Raychaudhuri, Tapan *Perceptions, Emotions, Sensibilities: Essays on Indian's Colonial and Post-colonial Experiences*, 1999, p. 5.

Sen, Amartya. *Argumentative Indian*, New Delhi, Oxford University Press. 2002.

Tagore, Rabindranath (henceforth RNT), 1921 "Letter to C.F. Andrews", published as 'Address on his 71st birthday', *Pravasi* (a vernacular journal), 1931

-RNT 1922, *An Eastern University in The English Writings of Rabindranath Tagore*, Volume 2 (henceforth EWRT 2), New Delhi Sahitya Akademi.

-Tagore and Geheeb, letter serial no. 131 entitled Paul and Edith Geheeb in Rabindra Bhavana archives, - Visva-Bharati.

- RNT's letter to his son, Rathindranath, 11 October, 1916, *Chithipatra*, Volume 2, Kolkata, Visva-Bharati Granthana Vibhaga.

-RNT, Letter dated 3rd November 1918, Rabindra Bhavana, Visva-Bharati archives, Serial No. 395.

-RNT, poem no. 35, *Gitanjali: Song Offerings*, Kolkata, Visva-Bharati Granthana Vibhaga. 2010.

-RNT, *Letters from Russia*, (vernacular text), 1931, included in the collected works, *Rabindra Rachanavali*, Vol. 10, Kolkata, Visva-Bharati Granthana Vibhaga. 1989.

Visva-Bharati University, see www.visva-bharati.ac.in

NOTES

1. Tagore's letter to C.F. Andrews, 1921.
2. RNT 1931, An address on his 71st birthday in Pravasi (a vernacular journal).
3. Amartya Sen 2002, Argumentative Indian, New Delhi, Oxford University Press
4. Anisuzzaman, 2012, 'Ihajagatika', in Ihajagatika O Ananya, p. 19.
5. RNT 1922, An Eastern University in The English Writings of Rabindranath Tagore, Volume 2 (henceforth EWRT2), pp. 556-569.
6. Tapan Raychaudhuri, Perceptions, Emotions, Sensibilities: Essays on Indian's Colonial and Post-colonial Experiences, 1999, p. 5.
7. RNT, 'The way to get it done' cited in Uma Dasgupta, Selected Writings on Education and Nationalism, 2009: 320.
8. Letters between Tagore and Geheeb, serial no. 131 entitled Paul and Edith Geheeb in Rabindra Bhavana archives, Visva-Bharati.
9. Martin Kaempchen, 2017-18, Rabindranath Tagore Meets Paul and Edith Geheeb: An Indo-German Encounter (project submitted to Indian Institute of Advanced Studies, Simla, India recently published, see bibliography. 20 Tagore and Social Work

10. 'Rabindranath Tagore in conversation with Romain Rolland', Amiya Chakravarty (ed.) Tagore Reader, accessed http://academic.udayton.edu/monishchatterjee/tagore/rolland.html (01.05.2019).
11. H.B. Mukherjee, 2013, Education for Fullness: A Study of the Educational Thoughts and Experiment of Rabindranath Tagore, India, Routledge, pp.419- 420. See also Kumkum Bhattacharya, 2014, Rabindranath Tagore: Adventure of Ideas and Innovative Practices in Education. Springer International. Pp 69-72.
12. RNT's letter to Rathindranath, 11 October, 1916, Chithipatra, Volume 2, pp. 55-56. Sabyasachi Bhattacharya, Rabindranath Tagore: An Interpretation, remarks, 'Anyone who has been to Los Angeles or the west coast of the United States would know that the idea was born in an appropriate place.' 2011, p.112.
13. Letter dated 3rd November 1918, Rabindra Bhavana, Visva-Bharati archives, Serial No. 395.
14. RNT, poem no. 35, Gitanjali: Song Offerings, 2010, p. 43.
15. For a more recent discourse on collective responsibility, see https://www.facebook.com/1500196238/posts/10220774186693416/?sfnsn=wiwspwa
16. Bhattacharya, Kumkum. 2012, "Utopias in Praxis: Rabindranath's Rural Reconstruction" in Utopias from Asia (An international and interdisciplinary symposium in Santiniketan on the occasion of the 150th birthday anniversary of Rabindranath Tagore edited by Konrad Meisig, Germany, Harrassowitz Verlag. Weisbaden
17. For details of Visva-Bharati University, see www.visva-bharati.ac.in
18. RNT, Letters from Russia, (vernacular text), 1931, included in the collected works, Rabindra Rachanavali, Vol. 10, 1989: 551-616.
19. Detailed discussion is available in Kumkum Bhattacharya 2014, Rabindranath Tagore: Adventure of Ideas and Innovative Practices in Education, Springer International.

2

Philosophy to Practice
Human Development and Social Work

I. Religious and Political Context

Rabindranath, though influenced by the nationalist movements, opened his mind at a very young age to various literary traditions, such as Arabo-Persian and European traditions, the latter including Shakespeare, Goethe, Schiller and Dante. The fascination of these great authors for the East heightened the interest of the young Bengali. It was the primary inspiration for his lifetime work of developing a universal thought system, in which Eastern and Western elements were interwoven. On reaching maturity, like most young Indians of important families, he studied in England, where he discovered a cultured, hospitable and affectionate people. There he found a civilized nation open to the world, completely at odds with his experience of the English living in India, who were scornful and, for the most part, racist towards Indians.

Arriving back in his home country in the 1890s, with British repression at its height[1], he took a stand against colonialism by writing a series of articles and by delivering numerous speeches in public. His lectures were already the premises of a new thought, being critical not only of the misdeeds of colonization, but also of the servility of the Indians, and of their propensity to defer to the decisions of those who govern them. At the same time, Tagore emphasised England's scientific and technical achievements, which were useful for the development of his country. Thus, he argued, the emancipation of India could not be achieved in opposition to the British Empire but rather from its indigenous forces, benefiting from the gains brought by the English Crown.

In 1904, Lord Curzon decided to divide the province of Bengal into two parts, one with a Muslim majority in the East, and the other with a Hindu majority in the West. Tagore responded publicly with a clear vision of the problems that would arise, involving problems in both Indian and English culture: the injustice of the caste system, the mutual contempt and mistrust between the two religious communities, and the erosion of peasant life. His speech, entitled *Swadeshi Samaj,* (Indigenous Society), appealed strongly to his compatriots. It developed the premises of a new social system: developing agriculture and supporting low-income farmers, protecting land tenants from the large landowners, educating children, organizing the health service, acquiring knowledge through popular access to culture, and elevating the status of local craftsmanship.

In 1905, in the context of the official partition of Bengal, he would put his words into effect, by making use of the ancestral constitution of village committees, putting at the head of each an interreligious duo comprising a member of the Hindu community together with a member of the Muslim community. These experiments led to the creation of joint funds to develop social, cultural and economic activities, leading in turn to the development of cooperative movements, as described in Chapter III.

The great novels of Tagore, such as *Gora* (1907), *The Home and the World* (1916), and *Four Chapters* (1934) allow one to grasp the complexity of the intellectual and political life of Bengal during the first half of the twentieth century. The questions they raised remain contemporary: the quest for identity and openness towards foreigners, the role and place of women in society, and the failure of the revolutionary ideals of nationalist or religious orders.

During these years of political commitment, the poet was hit hard by a period of family mourning. Within 5 years (1902–1907), he lost his wife Mrinalini in 1902, his second daughter, Renuka, aged 13 in 1903, his father Devendranath in 1905, and his younger son Shamindra, then also 13 years old, in 1907. Henceforth, he referred regularly to death in his poems. In the introduction to the *Song Offerings* (a translation of *Gitanjali*) Gide wrote: "All the last pieces of the *Gitanjali* are in praise of death. I do not think there is any other piece of literature with a more solemn and more beautiful tone" (Gide, 1925: XXXIII).

Tagore, driven by the search for unity, developed a strong quest for inner unity, undoubtedly nurtured by the pain he experienced, whether by the death of those near to him, or by the irrevocable partition of his region between Hindu and Muslim, imposed by the English.

Religious Spirit

The poet initiated an original line of thought underpinned by an inclusive vision, within which concepts conventionally regarded as dichotomous, were no longer mutually exclusive. He believed 'diversity and unity', 'identity and universality', 'Orient and Occident', do not oppose each other but enrich and cross-fertilise one another. He pleaded consistently for harmony between the two hemispheres, rejecting the colonial processes that monopolized power. Faced with the many divisions in India, the poet recalled that the immensity of this nation was built on the basis of the diversity of its people; that it had constantly been invaded. The ability to accept difference lay at the root of the greatness of a civilization that embraced cultural and religious diversity. All the religions present in India–Hinduism, Islam, Christianity, Buddhism, Jainism, Judaism and other tribes practicing animism–were themselves disparate, made of separatist movements, sects or specific doctrines. He liked to recall that every human being is but one element, one brick necessary for the construction of a much broader collective spirit that is nourished by differences. Revolutions demanding unjustified predominance of one person or group, driven by vanity, are obstacles to any collective development. To devote oneself to the whole does not require one to lose one's identity, but rather reinforces one's specific contribution to the collective task, in a pluralistic dynamic way supported by a unifying whole. This idea of universality has sometimes been misunderstood specially during the drive for India's liberation, a search for independence following several centuries of colonization. Wounded by grief, torn between his poetic aspirations and the political and social role forced on him by circumstance, Rabindranath Tagore sought inner peace. To this end, he disciplined himself to practice daily meditation. "His familiars attest, indeed, that everyday, at three o'clock in the morning, he would stand up and remain several hours in prayer. Sometimes, he would even spend several months in absolute solitude. His need to protect his inner life did not prevent him from being endowed with a prodigious faculty for work"[2] (Aslam, 1961: 16).

In a country like India, which is essentially religious and mystical, it was counter-productive to attempt to dissociate poetic inspiration from meditation, the poem from the prayer. The *Gitanjali* (Song Offerings) collection can be understood as essentially religious, but also philosophical; thoughts and writings which do not rely on a given school but aspire to be personal above all.

The poet's quest is to find God in himself. The mystery of life, the role of nature and peace of the soul, are at the origin of all oriental poetry and thought. It is from the beauty that transcends everyday trivialities that Rabindranath Tagore revitalizes himself.

His erudition and his sensitivity to aesthetics were the starting points of his writing, leading to a free literary style and to the many modes of artistic expression in which he excelled. The notion of the Supreme Being became more and more precise for him, and provided him with a key to the interpretation, even to the understanding of different worlds. However, in common with many Hindu philosophies, that of Tagore implies a renunciation, a rigorous asceticism. His posture remains open and serene, exalting life, nature, humanity and freedom: "In a word, the spirit of religion leads to freedom, its form to slavery" (Tagore, 1964: 184). In a spirit of universality and tolerance, Tagore speaks for the same God to whom all religions are directed, in different ways, be it Islam or Christianity, as well as different Hindu or Buddhist doctrines.

The Spirit of Educational Creativity

"Everywhere Oriental teaching has been reaffirmed in the judgment of those who had previously underestimated it. Its significant contribution to the evolution of human knowledge is recognized more and more every day." (*Ibid.*: 149) This quotation must be put in context in order to understand fully the scope of the message. The Indian elite in the 1900s recognised only Western education, thanks to the reputation of universities in England and the United States for the most part, which gained this recognition thanks to the advent of modern sciences and other modes of learning remote from classical oriental cultures.

This homogenisation of modes of learning, based on Western ideas, was seen as an immense loss in the eyes of the pedagogue and poet, even though he had benefited from the best English universities. Far from rejecting this system, Rabindranath welcomed the strength and intrinsic richness of the cultural exchange, and placed it at the heart of his plans for an international university, Visva-Bharati. Imagining such a university, one that would bring together knowledge from around the world in the Bengal of the early twentieth century, was a revolutionary idea in more ways than one. At a time when the eyes of the noteworthy and the Indian intelligentsia were turning to the West in their quest for new philosophical, cultural and technical knowledge, Tagore, making use of close friendships around the world, imagined a new university, combining empirical sciences with the arts, uniting openness to modernity and secular education to culture and nature. By transcending opposition while advancing the specific details, he planned to create a community of life open to all, regardless of national affiliation. As for the question of religion, Tagore sought spirituality beyond religious forms and his university would in this sense be secular. Thus, always anxious to unite abstract thought with concrete realization, he will draw a firm line on the issue of religious dogma within Visva-Bharati: "In this place, no image will be worshipped. And the faith of no man shall be despised." (Aslam, 1961: 73)

This educational project was driven by the force of his ideas, which aimed, by the juxtaposition of diversities, to neutralize excesses and bring out essential shared values, while preserving identities. Tagore conceived his educational model in an innovative spirit.

"Free the intelligence, and it will go forward." (Tagore, 1964: 153) The true function of a university is to keep the mind alert, the poet said, and "allow in the breadth of universal knowledge, especially when new ideas collide with old beliefs."(*Ibid.*: 153)

The project and then the realization of Visva-Bharati University was guided by the utopian concept of a gathering of intellectual, creative forces, driven by the idea that the resources of Eastern and Western thought, in their philosophical, economic and spiritual dimensions, would combine to open new perspectives, transcending territorial conflicts.

An educational centre that would develop a pure intelligence beyond the conflicts and the chaos that comes from competing national or international ideas. This university project was not inspired by the English models that Tagore had known in his youth, but by the great Buddhist training centres such as Nalanda[3] and Taxila.[4] It should be noted that the Government of India has now relaunched a university in Nalanda, as a place of cultural exchange and erudition for the East, the South-East and the South regions of Asia. The Nalanda mentor group, under the founding leadership of Dr. Amartya Sen, developed the project of a global university, seeking to create holistic thinking from the old and the new, the past, the present and the future. The university currently hosts three departments: History; Ecology and Environment; and Buddhist Studies, Philosophy and Comparative Religions.[5] Thus, it mirrors the universalist dimension of the pedagogue Tagore a century earlier.

"All peoples of the East and West can partake of learning and current knowledge. No one can afford to acquire science and learning in solitude. Thus history goes; science becomes universal, preparing the way for the intellectual unification of humanity." (*Ibid.*: 149)

The Spirit of Universalism

Throughout his life, Tagore remained close to his compatriots. He mixed with everyday life, observed injustice, put his eloquence to the service of just causes, fought to eliminate caste inequality, child marriages, and prejudice against women in Hindu society. But what worried him most, because of his broad view of the world, was the self-imposed confinement of peoples through the revival of nationalism. At the outbreak of the First World War 1914-1918, thanks to the fame he acquired following the award of the Nobel Prize for Literature (1913), he launched heartfelt messages of peace to the West. Tagore threw himself into an important mission, and despite his advanced age and the burdens linked with the development of his international university, he undertook long lecture tours in China, Japan, Europe and America.

"The same river of life that runs through my veins night and day runs around the world and dances in rhythmic pulsations."[6] (Aslam, 1961: 61)

He raised above all racial constraints and dreamed of harmony among all the people of the world. The East and the West were united in his mind in one and the same project of peace, without any risk of losing their diversity and unique characteristics which, far from contradicting one another, complement one another in a universalist spirit. While India ignited in a struggle for long-awaited independence, he concerned himself not only with the tensions between religions, but also with all that he saw as signs of future decadence[7] in Western civilization: its extreme materialism, the mechanization of a society that had moved away from its natural roots, the quest for instant gratification without regard to fundamental values. Without denying the usefulness of scientific progress, the poet, in love with a more spiritual and integrative life, sought to make the world of man conscious of its exact place in the Universe. This outlook, which would be defined today as emphasising sustainability, was a prophecy of the torments of the century to come.

Sometimes feeling isolated and alone, a common experience of people living ahead of their times, he sought refuge through writings which developed intellectual powers and humanist thinking, such as *Sadhana* (1916); *Nationalism* (1917); *Towards Universal Man* (1921); *The Religion of Man* (1931), all of which would find their pragmatic application in Visva-Bharati.

This vision of the world, dominated at the time by a secular oriental culture, was still unheard of among many Western thinkers who were seeking new ideas at the beginning of the 20th century. This quest for orientalism is still present today, in the 21st century, through the renewed interest in various techniques such as yoga, Ayurvedic massages, meditation or the classical dance of South India. Already, in 1911, Rabindranath raised the question of the accelerated opening of communications between peoples and nations. "Today there is widespread communication among the different peoples of the world. International contacts are multiplying. One might have thought, therefore, that time had come to bury racial and national differences. And yet, by a strange paradox, separatism between nations is strengthened as the doors open more widely to the outside world, and the obstacles to communication disappear. It seemed at one time that men were separated from each another because the means for relationships were lacking. This lack no longer applies, yet separation persists." (Tagore, 1964, 143).

We must remember that at the time of these remarks there were no mobile phones or computers, and international airlines were reserved for politicians and wealthy businessmen. This analysis can be applied without comment to our contemporary epoch, which is defined as the era of communication. A century later, the similarity of analysis remains unsettling.

The poet philosopher described what was at stake for the planet based on the experience of his many travels as well as the wisdom of the secular writings of Hindu philosophy. He thus evoked a modernity of purpose that still persists today. "The problem around the world today is to be able to achieve unity, not by erasing all differences, but by maintaining them; it is a difficult task because there are no short cuts, but rather a need for generosity of exchanges. However, what seems easy is not always easy to accomplish, whereas, over time, difficult tasks prove easy." (*Ibid.*: 147)

Thanks to his universalist spirit, he met many Western thinkers, and Romain Rolland was one of the closest. In addition to a few visits which Tagore undertook to Switzerland, to Villeneuve where Romain Rolland and his wife had taken refuge, the two great internationalists maintained a close friendship for many years via correspondence.[8]

At the beginning of the 20th century, most nations were becoming aware of their ties with mankind as a whole. At the same time, and perhaps in tandem, they struggled to preserve their own identity. Through this emerging awareness, they were partly able to shake off those attributes that constituted an obstacle to connect with the outside world. But for each one, in the depths of their consciousness, there remained a tendency to isolate themselves from humanity as a whole through emphasising their particular attributes. These conflicting tendencies of opening up and shutting off ultimately resulted in negation, an insistence on the importance of some kind of hegemony in the face of an uncertain future that reached its tragic destiny with the outbreak of the First World War.

Following his many journeys, Tagore advocated a universalist spirit as the only way to foil the fantasies of the great dictators in power at that time.

However, understanding the poet philosopher's message required a move away from the Western philosophies that emphasised dualities. For Tagore, the Universe was one and multiple. The challenge, through education, was to rise above a way of living that barricaded itself from all things foreign, while preserving the diversity of ways of life and ways of belonging to the world, emphasising the diversity of the world and of nature. "Thus we find that it is Unity which expresses itself through creation, and the Multitude which, by its contrasts, completes the revelation of unity." (Tagore, [1924] 2015: 19)

During the First World War, the image of Europe as a constructive, ingenious and avant-garde force suffered its worst setback. The failings in terms of humanity, the exclusion and the sacrifices demanded by national egotism, eclipsed its proven capacity to modernize through industrialization. The myth of achieving a better life through the personal acquisition of material goods outweighed the quest for the common good; if not to collectively defend themselves against a potential enemy, people fought to protect their accumulated wealth. This defensive attitude created a posture of exclusion, rejection, out of fear of defeat. If there were many voices raised at the international level, supported by thinkers who embraced peace and universality, the spirit of freedom in the masses was expressed in a need to defend themselves against the enemy by the armament of nations, by a frantic struggle to acquire new territories, a sign of future wealth and security.

During his many speeches, the poet's voice appeared derisory or coming from another age, when he passionately evoked the urgency of raising man's thoughts above the level of material attractions.

"Truth confers unity but wealth brings disunity." (Tagore, 1964: 230) Faced with the rise of nationalism in Germany and Italy, the universalists argued for the need for open borders and the advantages of abandoning approaches that impeded the achievement of the long-term good. "The day has come when it is no longer possible to call nationalism anything more than the spirit of steeple. Under penalty of incurring the enduring condemnation of Humanity, we must divest ourselves of all the prejudices and customs which keep us isolated behind artificial barriers, barriers which oppose movement to thought, to action." (*Ibid.*: 155) and again "The institutions we create today express both our national feeling and our cosmopolitan sense." (*Ibid.*: 156)

The Spirit of Unity and Diversity

Beyond the beauty of his prose, the poet's writings expressed concern about the loss of the very idea of unity. He warned against the pernicious danger of wanting to achieve unity at all costs when the foundations for that task were not laid down and understood as bringing added value for all. "A separation that we try to suppress has a terrible explosive force: at any moment it can give rise to a formidable upheaval, exploding under the pressure imposed on it. The best way to Union is to respect the separation of what is in reality separate reality. It is only when man is conscious of his individuality that he aspires to grow. Without this feeling, it is lost in the mass. Every entity, no matter how small, as soon as it becomes conscious of its personality, seeks to preserve it–such is the law of life. It prefers to live within its limits than to die in bloom." (Tagore, 1964: 144).

True unity stems from the harmony between natural differences. The poet made us aware that an artificial uniformity, or even standardization by dictat, stultifies creativity. Conversely, intellectual cooperation and the development of knowledge through comparative study that respects diversity are the cornerstones of a globalized future. Undissociated unity and diversity open perspectives of thought respectful of difference and of mutual enrichment.

"Unity among men becomes a possibility only at this level of grandeur. Unity in misery or subjection, union imposed by force, is only an illusory union". (*Ibid.*: 145) The reduction of differences down to a shapeless mass cannot produce progress for all, the long-term good stems from the enrichment of individual personalities.

The philosophy, derived from the Hindu religion defines separateness, and even opposition, as a means of achieving unity. The search for Truth involves the acceptance of opposing controversies that mark the opening to an evolution of thought. Without this sinuous path, Truth, which is always partial, cannot be attained, as it requires a process to recognize gaps, the errors of judgment, and the incompleteness of all thought. The quest for truth is reflected in human relationships, which are enriched by the confrontation of differences, not through a struggle to prove others wrong or gain power over them, but through a willingness to open up, grasping other possible paths, new unsuspected horizons, stemming from diversity.

Rabindranath Tagore, deeply affected by the emerging world war, defined Western civilization as a perpetual quest for truth between good and evil, which knows no conciliation except victory or defeat. He was alarmed by the creation of a border between East and West, not on the ground but through different ways of conceiving and understanding life, based on exclusion instead of acceptance of differences.

For the thinker, the quest for the truth of existence derives its creative energy from diversity, moving towards unity. The truth of unity approaches perfection through the fact that it is the relative of union. Thus truth, as conceived by the wise through long meditation, emphasized the quest for unity in all things. Unity achieved through global understanding of the strength of diversity, the beauty engendered by the harmony of differences, such as the rainbow, which illuminates the sky by the multiplicity of its colours. A unity in diversity, which moves away from the processes of uniformity.

Tagore draws his inspiration from his own culture without denying the contribution of diverse knowledge derived from many different practices and customs. In his message on the link between East and West, he does not seek to articulate the differences between two cultures, but to emphasize the richness of a universal wisdom. It is the link between East and West in the incessant circle of the sun and the earth that best conveys his message. Epistemology far removed from an India enfeebled by several centuries of domination, be it that of the Nabobs or the British. Rather than suggesting a single connection, the poet thinker retains the possibility of multiple pathways. Moving beyond the chasm between a dominating West and a dominated East, Tagore invites us to adopt a different perspective or, more precisely, he insists on the need for a transformation of our point of view. We can reflect that in our global, cosmopolitan era, East and West should no longer be viewed as separate entities, that they are infinitely intertwined. These words describe goals that are actually unattainable, for we are always East or West of a given point. But the present construction of a cosmopolitan world retains little of the message of the great thinkers who have marked our way of life. The strength of exchange through the ties of love and thought is cast aside in the crude world of materialism, the struggle of economic conquest and the endless search for monetary gain.

The Spirit of Harmony

"In our ancient literature, the hermitage shines as a link between man and the rest of creation, hitherto separated by an abyss. In the tragedies of Western theatre, human characters attract our attention by their fiery passions" (Tagore, 2015: 67). In the *Ramayana*, the greatness of the hero is not defined by a bitter struggle with Nature, but by his sympathy towards it. This rapport with the holistic world develops step by step in the farthest corners of the world, under the aegis of a new model linking humanity to Planet Earth, through the concept of sustainable development. A link to renewed nature is established, not by treating it as alien and seeking to dominate it, but by understanding it as a whole, of which we are a part, in uniting ourselves to it in the most universal possible communion. Ancient India does not deny the superiority of man, but the proof of this superiority lies in the extent of his compassion, rather than in from a remote, overbearing attitude, driven by discrimination and domination.

The way of looking at the world, as articulated by ancestral writings, can be summarized by the Sanskrit word *Sachidananda*. It means that Reality, which is essentially one, has three phases. The first is *Sat*: the simple fact that things are. This fact unites us to all things through our common existence. The second is *Chit*: knowing. This fact unites us to all things through knowledge. Finally, the third is *Ananda*: enjoyment. This fact unites us to all things through the medium of love. (*Ibid.*: 65)

Thus, the Sanskrit word for Truth literally means "what exists"– "Sat". This relationship between the fact of being present, in a certain materiality, of opening oneself to the knowledge of the things that surround us, and of reaching out to enjoy them, returns to the central idea of harmony. The ultimate goal is not to live in this world, to know it and to use it, but, by coupling the three elements, for each human being, to realize his own unity by expanding his compassion. The strength of inner freedom, exalted by the harmony derived from the rich variety of forms in nature, from its rhythms, from human activity, from relations with others, in creativity and knowledge, allow us to progress towards true unity. The ideal of harmony, which can be understood as the culmination of diversity in unity, is not an abstract notion but a real personal experience and an intuition that accompanied Tagore throughout his life.

A position that unites the relation between oneself and others, in an active contextuality[9], where one experiences, through the feeling of unity, this deep pleasure of the hospitality that Life offers to life. The idea of diversity in unity is certainly a working concept in the moral, social and aesthetic order, and one which is so necessary when faced with the chaos of our present world. We can relate this sensibility to the weaving of bonds, to the idea of *complex thought*, as defined in Europe today by the illustrious philosopher Edgar Morin. Complexity is "a fabric (complexus: what is woven together of heterogeneous constituents inseparably associated: it poses the paradox of the one and the multiple." (Morin, 2005: 21) As we have seen, in Eastern culture, the one and the multiple lead us to the notion of multiplicity and unity, which are not experienced as a paradox but as a truth to be apprehended, with a view to freedom of being, to the attainment of harmony. The central idea is to see in each culture, in each collective entity, in each person, an intrinsic variety that produces different levels of unity. This means going beyond the practice of promoting one culture by opposing other types of expression. Tagore writes and speaks in favour of a universal culture which is made up of a multitude of approaches which, in their achievement, contribute to the nourishment of mankind. A true unity, respectful and open to the diversity of cultures, which rejects all forms of uniformity imposed by power and domination. He believed in the unity of India, in its diversity of cultures and religions, and he believed incontrovertibly that this plurality formed a harmonious and creative force.

Tagore was also disturbed by the risk of division within nations, between the growing wealth and rampant poverty. He prophesied, in terms of today's world, as follows: "But excessive inequality is equally harmful since it greatly impedes social contacts between men by the obstacles it raises between them. Evil builds its nest in the shadow of these obstacles."(*Ibid.*: 313) Once again, he speaks of a pervasive reality. The accomplishment of wealth lies in the very idea of accumulation. The desire to possess ever more, is materialized today by a vertiginous increase of the wealth of a small number to the detriment of ever more glaring black spots of poverty. The fulfilment of a life is achieved from social ties that are woven through cooperation and recognition of the strength of a diversity that unites us.

He placed hope in the democracy of the West, but he also saw its limits with the arrival of the first and the preparation of the Second World War.[10] As he saw it, if pluralism really exists in all living systems, then conflicts must arise from defects in humans of cultural understanding. The problems are not only psychological and institutional constructs, but arise also from contextual issues. The elevation of thought, through an education open to harmony, whether by the example of nature, through culture, or through artistic creativity (song, dance, poetry, arts) is the basis of transcendence, which opens the access to immanence. Man grows not only through his ties with his loved ones, but also through the environmental context that forms his perceptions of the world. The goal of a life can be seen as a double revolution, that of developing one's own psyche, on the one hand, and of overcoming the inequitable social structures, on the other. It becomes possible to overcome one's own fears, drawing inspiration from the harmony that asserts itself when one opens one's heart and soul to the wonder and the joy that this gives.

The Spirit of Joy and Simplicity

The poet believed in the possible realization of an elevation of thought not only for a pacifist understanding of the world, but to bring a fundamental element to the completeness of mankind through the feeling of joy. Gide, in his introduction to the Lyric Offering, would retain this essential element.

"*When the perception of this perfection of unity,*" says Rabindranath Tagore in another place of Sadhana, "*is not purely intellectual, when it opens us up to the luminous consciousness of totality, joy radiates, love spreads over everything.*" (Gide, 1925: XXXII) Tagore perceived that the remoteness of his international university, far from the hustle and bustle of cities, would have the advantage of keeping a proper distance from the events of social and political life. Retreat made it possible to accept people as they came, without having to make them conform to prevailing ideas, and thus to consider them in a reasonable perspective. For him the most important consideration was the search for a universal truth, which is arrived at by opening the doors to the unknown, to what exists beyond appearances and the certainties that stem from tradition or fear of the unknown. Acknowledging what may seem distant from oneself is essential for a free mind. In preparation for a voyage to the West, the poet recalled that realities are rarely visible to the naked eye. Especially in opulent countries, where they are "not hidden by rags, but by veils of brilliant illusion which make them even more difficult to perceive" (Tagore, 1964: 159).

He relied on the strength of the West, speaking of experimentation and constant evolution, perpetual change that is not driven by a search for escape, but is accompanied by an open and adventurous spirit that transforms and transcends certainties. He reminds us that it is the vital force of the tree that causes it to lose its dead leaves and renew them. Journeys are, in a sense, a pilgrimage to the Truth, overcoming the obstacles, the pain resulting from establishing contact in difficult contexts. Relations with others depend on the love we can bring to others, "(....) love, which is the power of the Spirit, infinite patience and joyful devotion." (Tagore, 1964, 167). Such a posture requires us to be able to strip ourselves of our own self-sufficiency, to emerge from the illusory, knowing that true wisdom requires a greater awareness of our own finitude. His work, *Sadhana*, bears the mark of this life project. "The side of our existence which faces the infinite does not aspire to opulence but to freedom, to joy. The reign of need ceases, so that our function is not to possess but to be. To be what? To be one with Brahma, for the religion of the infinite is the religion of unity......" (Gide, 1925: XXX).

Tagore refused to recognize the merit of poverty when it is only seen as a negation. To place asceticism in opposition to luxury would be to fight one evil by another. Under no circumstances should poverty and simplicity be confused. Simplicity had a value in itself, it should not lead to a lack in essential goods that would impoverish communities, it is a sign of perfection. It was through a lack of simplicity that the superfluous had invaded our daily lives, demanding a productivity which crushed the working masses for the profit of a few. The same was true of the necessities of life themselves, which were becoming more and more costly. It was not a question of preaching the worship of a simple life by glorifying the spiritual merits of poverty. It advocates a more sensitive approach, emphasising the joy we feel when we detach ourselves from our attraction to the superficial. "It is insensitivity which deprives us of our simple power of enjoyment and condemns us, through pretentious snobbery, to be proud of absurd and costly expenditure." (Tagore, 1964, 275).

Social and Educational Goals

"Uniformity is not unity. Only those who differ can unite."[11] It is by recognizing the individuality of individuals, groups or nations, in terms of the issues and positions in which they differ, that a true unity is approached, where a pluralist agreement can be found. Openness to exchange is in our primordial roots, not to conquer, but to share that which contributes to achievement of self-awareness. "He who recognizes others in himself and himself in others does not remain unknown to himself." (Tagore, 1964, 231); an adage drawn from the Upanishads which should, according to the thinker, be the motto of any educational institution. And again, "He who has understood the uniqueness of humanity by identifying himself with the universe has freed himself from ignorance and suffering." (Tagore, 1964: 235, Isa Upanishad: 6)

Through Tagore's words, we find the ancient message of India, that the One and the Indivisible is peaceful and eternal. This is the Doctrine of the *Advaita*, which expounds non-dualism, a school of Vedantic philosophy which reached its apogee in the era of Shankaracharya, around the ninth century.[12]

Tagore devoted his life to reviving these fundamental precepts, whether through his poetry, his novels or more explicitly, in his humanist essays. Convinced of the need to link thought to action, as promoted by the pragmatism of the philosopher Dewey, a contemporary of Tagore, he created an educational centre where the peoples of all countries could meet in the search for truth, a harmonious development of the destiny of men. It was his way of laying a foundation stone in the construction of world peace.

Today's social issues are derived from broad universal themes that we find difficult to tease out, because the factors related to the relevant situations intersect. Psychosocial issues, exclusion, the rise of radicalism, poverty, vulnerability, isolation and loneliness, the various forms of forced migration, the lack of social cohesion, multiple forms of dependency, disability and the aging of the population, to name but a few, transcend national borders. Social intervention today is based on the grand precepts of participation, inclusion, citizenship, and the empowerment and autonomy of people in need of support.

Behind this set of multi-referential variables which has long been described as problematic, because it is dispersed, without clear boundaries and therefore not very amenable to precise and predetermined objectives, a pluralistic reading offers a postmodern approach, a model of thought and intervention that is complex or hybrid, based on plasticity and homeostasis. Emergence from a simplistic vision, or from a deterministic framework, forces us to think on the basis of complexity and paradoxes, which at times seem to us beyond our grasp. It is here that Rabindranath Tagore's philosophy can be immensely supportive, since his holistic vision, driven by the concepts of diversity, unity and truth in their harmonious relationship with the universe around us, allows us to enter into the complexity by going off the beaten track and restoring all the strength and beauty of what connects, rather than what differentiates. Reflection on the problems of exclusion allows us to go beyond divisions and to enter into a pragmatic model, based on diversity that allows us to recognize each entity as part of a universal and inclusive vision.

Deconstructing the dual representations of our world, between good and evil, between the worker and the businessman, between civilization and nature, between respect for tradition and the contribution of innovation, leads to a linear, simplistic and judgmental thought. The advance of civilization and new means of communication contribute their share of difficulties which require systematic understanding. Paradoxes are everywhere, but the real breakthrough lies in the way we apprehend them and work with them, for ourselves and for others. In this, Tagore's thought is an invaluable source of inspiration.

BIBLIOGRAPHICAL REFERENCES

Aslam, O., 1961, *Rabindranath Tagore*, Paris, Editions Pierre Seghers.
Morin, E., 1990, *Introduction à la pensée complexe,* Paris, Seuil.
Morin, E., 2016, *Pour une crisologie,* Paris, L'Herne.
Rolland, R., 1960, *Inde Journal, 1915–1943*, Paris, Albin Michel.
Tagore, R., [1924] 2015, *La religion du poète*, Paris, Payot & Rivages.
Tagore, R., 1964, *Vers l'homme universel,* Paris, Gallimard nrf.
Tagore, R., Traduction de Gide A., 1925, *L'Offrande Lyrique*, Paris, Editions Gallimard nrf.

NOTES

1. Indian Council Act: the manipulation of the pound's currency rate exchange to the detriment of the rupee; Sedition Bill in 1986 forbidding any kind of protest.

2. Aslam O., 1961, *Rabindranath Tagore*, Paris, Editions Pierre Seghers.
3. Nalanda University was a major centre of Hindu thinking, mainly Buddhist, its influence stretched over the greater part of Central Asia, the Himalayas, South-East Asia and Japan. See: e Cornu Ph., *Dictionnaire encyclopédique du Bouddhisme*, Seuil, New Edition 2006.
4. Taxila was a centre of ancient Buddhist studies from 4th century B.C. to the 2nd century. Nowadays, it is designated as a World Heritage Site, located in the Punjab province of Pakistan. It was well known on the Silk Road, and would draw students from all-over the ancient Buddhist world.
5. Several international personalities, such as the Nobel laureate Amartya Sen, George Yeo, the former Foreign Minister of Singapore, Sugata Bose of Harvard University, Lord Meghnad Desai of the London School of Economics and other dignitaries have been involved with Nalanda University since its founding.
6. Poem LXIX, in Tagore R. 1917, *L'offrande Lyrique*, translated by André Gide, Paris, Edition de la Nouvelle revue française, p. 97.
7. See Odette Aslam: Livre sur le Nationalisme (excerpt) p. 187, Crépuscule du siècle, p. 189.
8. See *Inde-Journal*, 1915-1943 by Romain Rolland (1960).
9. Reference to his work: *La Maison et le Monde*.
10. Reference to his work: *La Maison et le Monde*.
11. Tagore, 1964, *Towards Universal Man*, 233.
12. *Vers l'Homme universel*, p. 236.

3

Tagore and Social Work[1]

Social work is as old as humanism, Buddhism, Hinduism and Christianity. Nevertheless, its formal growth as a profession could be marked in the later part of 19th century in the United States and the United Kingdom. The growth of social work as an education in India began in the early 20th century while Bombay Social Service League initiated training of the voluntary worker interested in serving the poor and the vulnerable. However, in 1936 with the establishment of the erstwhile Sir Dorabji Tata Graduate School of Social Work, (now Tata Institute of Social Sciences) in Mumbai to train personnel for social welfare made the beginning of professional social work education at the post-graduate level. Since 1947 institutions offering social work at the post-graduate and graduate level (1963), have emerged in different parts of the country. Mahatma Gandhi Kashi Vidyapeeth, Delhi School of Social Work, Madras School of Social Work, Indore School of Social Work are among the followers to introduce social work education at the post-graduate level. The Department of Social Work, Visva-Bharati is one among the first institutes that initiated a course at the under-graduate level (1963), post-graduate and Ph.D. (1977) and remained as the only one institute in the Eastern India until the 1990s.

The roots of social work in India lay in the history of tradition–the concept of 'service to the society' that existed in different forms and the contributions made by noted social thinkers and social reformers.

Social work aims at promoting human welfare through prevention and relief to the sufferers. Its special concern has always been with human problems of living. According to the International Federation of Social Workers (2014), "Social work is a practice-based profession and an academic discipline that promotes social change and development, social cohesion, and the empowerment and liberation of people. Principles of social justice, human rights, collective responsibility and respect for diversities are central to social work. Underpinned by theories of social work, social sciences, humanities and indigenous knowledge, social work engages people and structures to address life challenges and enhance well-being. The above definition may be amplified at national and/or regional levels."[2]

Social work in its various forms addresses the multitude, complex interactions between people and their environments. The missions are to enable all people to develop their full potential, enrich their lives and prevent dysfunction. Professional social work is focused on problem solving and change. As such, social workers are change agents in society and in the lives of the individuals, families and communities they serve.

The practice of social work addresses the barriers, inequalities and injustices that exist in society. It responds to crises and emergencies as well as to everyday personal and social problems. Social work utilizes a variety of skills, techniques and activities consistent with its holistic focus on persons and their environment. Social work interventions range from primarily person-focused psychosocial processes to involvement in social policy, planning and development. Those include counseling, clinical social work, group work, social pedagogical work, and family treatment and therapy as well as efforts to help people obtain services and resources in the community through organization and development initiatives as macro-practice. Interventions include agency administration, community organizations and engaging in social and political action to impact social policy and economic development. The holistic focus of social work is universal, but the priorities of social work vary from country to country, region to region and from time to time depending on cultural, historical and socio-economic conditions.

The concept of social work given by G.R. Banerjee is a good framework to understand social work. "Social work can be regarded as an organized effort of the society to help effect the wholeness of man, i.e., his maximum growth in all aspects–physical, social, emotional, intellectual, cultural, moral and spiritual–so that he can adjust better to all or any part of the total environment or modify the environment for better adjustment. This effort is carried out by means of guiding, and various other problem solving activities with individuals alone or in groups and also by social reform i.e., reform of the conditions that create social ills. The social worker here is taken as a person who is at the service of human beings in order to help them to self-realization and development" (1964).

There is an oft-repeated criticism that professional social work in India has been heavily influenced by Western concepts and practice. There are some efforts to show the continuity between traditional Indian values and the values of professional social work (Banerjee, 1975[3], Wadia, 1961[4]). Rabindranath Tagore was one among them, whose versatility towards rural reconstruction is widely acknowledged in India and abroad. There is no branch of literature that he has not touched and enriched. Tagore, however, did not dwell exclusively in the realm of ideas. He gave free reins to his imagination through music, dance and painting, yet never lost contact with the more immediate problems around him. One can regard Tagore as the father of the movement of rural resuscitation in India. He became an ardent advocate of a thorough reconstruction of rural life at least a generation before the Indian National Congress turned its attention in this direction. The poet was the first to plead for a constructive policy. In the days of the anti-partition movement in Bengal, he more than anybody else, stirred patriotic feelings through his songs and speeches and writings. Yet he never ceased to stress the imperative need to harness the rising tide of emotion to some creative enterprise for the benefit of the country. The train would never make any progress, he argued, if its engine continued to whistle away all its steam (Sen, 1991:64).[5] He is one such social philosopher who could visualize the past, present and future of the people and the country needing help and assistance to prevent, encounter and build a better India by organizing the rural communities with its inner strength. His observation and experiences in India, Europe and America convinced him to unite the poor and vulnerable groups first and educate them on the trade they wished.

Tagore and Social Work

To begin with we would like to take a look at how Rabindranath conceptualized 'social work' in his thoughts and then discuss his values and concepts relevant to the profession of social work. There is no explicit mention of the word 'social work' in the works of Tagore in the sense that is understood today. A close approximation used by Tagore to explain social worker is '*Visvakarma*' (worker of the world) and social work is '*Visvakarma*' (worker of the world) Banerjee (1966). The other instance where one comes across the term social worker in Tagore's work is in relation to the administration of services from Sriniketan. The workers who were posted in the villages were called *samaj karmis* or social workers and the more senior ones were known as *kendra karmis* or centre workers. The *gram karmi* or village worker was placed in charge of each smaller unit and the *kendra karmi* took charge of larger units that federated a number of small orbits of villages. The social worker even though was placed at the end of the organizational hierarchy, was given great significance as he was considered as the institute's mouthpiece in the village and the success of the programme depended on the performance of the social worker.

The importance given to the worker by Tagore explains the professionalism in this approach. The first objective of Sriniketan as enumerated by Tagore is explicit about the need to develop a professional relationship with the community–"To win the friendship and affection of villagers and cultivators by taking a real interest in all concerning their life and welfare, and by making a lively effort to assist them in solving their most pressing problems". Similar efforts in settlement house movement could be traced in 1884 in London and Hull House in Chicago in 1889 where the volunteers settled in communities to improve the life and living of the vulnerable people. Here, in Sriniketan experiment, the workers were asked to live in the villages, come in close touch with people realizing that the village is not merely an intellectual problem, but 'a living being'. Thus the worker–community relationship is qualified on the basis of being genuine, warm, respectful and purposeful. With regards to the process of community work, the workers were instructed to work with the people and neither 'for them' nor 'on behalf of them', but not in isolation. His efforts were to mobilize the people, so that they could build their own leadership and institutions and make an effective use of the services provided at the institute for solution of their problems. He was to act as the peoples' agent, interpreting people's problems to the experts so that the planning was democratic and not superimposed from the top. He was not to distribute material benefits but to help the villagers to make an efficient use of modern resources for the improvement of their total cultural conditions. (Dasgupta, 1962: 34-35)[6] People's participation and self-help was thus advocated in the process of community work which is the core idea of community organization in social work.

Tagore also reflected on the professional and personal self of the social worker. According to him, the worker must possess a balanced personality, instinctive humanity, infinite amount of tact and patience and adequate insight into human nature (*Ibid*.: 35).[7] In his essay *Spiritual Union*, he explains some of the qualities of the social worker. To quote: "In order to be united with Him we have to divest our work of selfishness and become *Visvakarma*, meaning 'the world worker', we must work for all. When I use the words 'for all', I do not mean for a countless number of individuals. All work that is good, however small in extent, is universal in character. Such work makes for a realization of *Visvakarma*, 'The World-Worker' who works for all. In order to be one with the *Maha Atma*, 'The Great Soul', one must cultivate the greatness of soul which identifies itself with the soul of all people and not merely with that of one's own"[8] (Tagore, 2000:41).

According to Tagore, social work should thus carry two essential features; it should work that serves the interest of the community in a micro sense and secondly; it should be altruistic in nature. While speaking on '*Visvakarma*', Tagore gave prime concern to work done with the community as a whole that would lead to the welfare of the individual. Tagore had recognized the importance of communal life in the East contrary to the individualistic society of West. His concern from micro to macro perspectives of development can be understood from his concern for Bengal. He believed that all constructive activities must start from one's own immediate environment. He repeatedly stressed that political and social workers must concentrate on their neighbourhood. He used to say that if even one village could carry out the programme he had visualized, it would act like a lamp from which light could radiate in all direction (Kabir, 1961:32).[9] Evidently, the main point of interest in Tagore's thoughts on social work was the community and community welfare. The idea at the core of this approach was that in the welfare of the whole society laid on the welfare of the individuals but not *vice versa*. One could interpret this as development social work in the modern terminology.

The second essential feature refers to the social worker as a selfless and fair-minded person (Banerjee, 1966:41). Tagore accorded high approbation to voluntary workers who discharge their deeds without expecting any return and for the mere love of the work. This, however, does not eliminate paid professional workers from the purview of the 'world-worker'. The acceptance of remuneration does not necessarily detract the paid worker from the value of his work. On the other hand, he enjoys economic security that a voluntary worker in contrast does not enjoy. What matters really is whether the work is done devotedly and sincerely. Disinterested services should, therefore, be construed to mean service, which is rendered sincerely with a view of benefiting the party who receives it.

Philosophy, Values of Social Work and Tagore

The practice of social work is deeply rooted in philosophy and human values. Values are problem preventing while skills are problem solving. Values are concerned with becoming, for instance, becoming a good social worker. Skills deal with doing, the way we practice social work, but skills do not address moral and ethical issues. Hence, it is important to find a right balance between values and skills. In the classical essay on social work's values, Gordon (1965) argues that for a social worker 'to value' something is to 'prefer it'. A measure of the extent of a preference is what price, effort or sacrifice one will make to obtain what is preferred, whether article, behaviour or state of affairs. To identify a value held by an individual or a society, therefore, requires a description of "what is preferred and some measure of the extent of that preference, that is, the price in effort, money or sacrifice the individual will pay to achieve his preference, or the provision a society will make or the positive or negative sanction it will impose to enforce the preference".

When Rabindranath speaks of values, he does not concern himself with what are known as pragmatic values. Such values are extrinsic that can be measured by a rational standard; he neither denies their existence. But real values, according to him, are intrinsic values that fall within the scope of intuition and not reason. To say intrinsic values fall within the province of intuition is not to say that they are meaningless. The fact that a large number of people use these values successfully in everyday life is a presumption that these values are used meaningfully. These values are not meant for describing any natural phenomena. So their meaningfulness cannot be measured by logical analysis. But they have a meaning of their own, entail a kind of behaviour on the part of persons who use them. If one goes through the vast writing by the poet, one finds that he takes up a problem, analyzes its contents empirically and tries to arrive at a solution (Ray, 1961:193).[10]

According to Rabindranath, values have an objective reality of their own. He declares that man does not create values, but only discovers and realizes them. "In our life we have one side which is infinite, where we exhaust ourselves at every step, and we have another side, where our aspirations, enjoyment and sacrifice are infinite. This infinite side of man must have its manifestation in some symbols, which have the element of immortality. Therefore, it refuses all that is flimsy and feeble and incongruous. It builds for its dwelling a paradise, where only those materials are used that have transcended the earth's mortality". When man discovers infinite in him, he discovers the realm of values. He believes in Truth (*Satya*), Beauty (*Sundara*), Goodness (*Siva*), Bliss (*Ananda*) and similar values. Also he believes that all values culminate in the grand value of *Ananda.* Truth, Beauty, Goodness and Bliss belong to the infinite side of man's nature. Mere discovery of values is not enough. They must also be realized. To realize values is to realize infinite personality in us. Intrinsic values are end in themselves while extrinsic values are means to the ends, which are valued. Strictly speaking, according to the poet, there is only one supreme value namely *Ananda* (Bliss) which express itself in and through other values.

Social workers have always embraced a core set of values. Social work grew out of humanitarian and democratic values and its values are based on respect for equality, worth and dignity of all human beings. Since its beginning, social work practice has focused on meeting human needs and developing human potential. Human rights and social justice serve as the motivational and justification for social work action. In solidarity with those who are disadvantaged, the profession strives to alleviate poverty and to liberate vulnerable and oppressed people in order to promote social inclusion. Social work values are embodied in the professional code of ethics. Frederic (1997: 346)[11] summarizes the commonly cited work values by different authors as individual worth and dignity, respect for persons, self-determination, the importance of human relationships, professional integrity, social justice, valuing individual's capacity to change, providing individuals with opportunity to change, seeking to provide individuals with adequate resources and services to meet their needs, empowerment, confidentially and privacy, equal opportunity, organizational loyalty and non-discrimination.

Consistent with the profession's historic and contemporary commitment to serving populations that are vulnerable and oppressed, the preamble of the National Association of Social Workers (NASW) Code of Ethics (1996)[12] states, "The primary objective of the social work profession is to enhance human well-being and help achieve basic human needs for all people, with particular attention to the needs and empowerment of people who are vulnerable, oppressed and living in poverty." A historic and defining feature of social work is the profession's focus on individual well-being in a social context and the well-being of society. Fundamental to social work is attention to the environmental forces that create, contribute and address problems in living....the mission of the social work profession is rooted in a set of core values. These core values, embraced by social workers throughout the profession's history are the foundation of social work's unique purpose and perspective. They include service, social justice, dignity and worth of the person, importance of human relationships, integrity and competence.

The Code of Ethics for professional social workers in India spells out the value framework for the worker, the profession and the society as follows:

1. I pledge to perceive people as having inherent worth and dignity, irrespective of their attributes and achievements and having the capability of continuing development; I pledge to perceive myself and other people as part of nature, needing to live in harmony with other non-human existence.
2. I pledge to work towards the overall well-being of people in spirit of *Sarvodaya* (rise of all the people), through the achievements of the following goals: Equity, non-hierarchy and non-discrimination of human groups in terms of race, religion, tribe, language, regional origin, gender, sexual orientation and other such factors and condemning segregation/apartheid/discrimination among them; Social, economic, political and legal justice, ensuring satisfaction of basic needs integrity and security, universal access to essential

resources and protective safeguards for the marginalized people; and people-centred development, in the spirit of *Swarajya* (Self-governance) and democracy from micro to macro levels, where people participate to determine their life styles and goals for development.

3. I pledge to work with people, guided by the following values; Solidarity and partnership with the marginalized people and; Peaceful and non-violent approaches in the spirit of *Ahimsa* for resolving conflicts with self, other and the environment (TISS, 1997).

Having mentioned the value orientation, related to international and national commitments, let us now look into some of the values and concepts of social work as they relate to Tagore's ideal of rural reconstruction. In his programme of constructive work Tagore laid the greatest stress on the improvement of village life. He considered this as the most promising field for nation-building activities that was also the field in which the need for patriotic enterprise was most pressing. Tagore's idea of nationalism as mentioned in the earlier chapters are in contrast to the more sectarian notions. In his writings on political and social problems, he came back and again to this theme. This is particularly true in his stream of essays in the beginning of the 20th century, especially during the anti-partition movements. His thoughts on village problems when put together give us a complete picture of his ideal of rural life as also of the methods on which he relied for its realization. His rare insight into the problems of rural India, the comprehensive nature of recommendations and the transparent idealism which underlies them–together give social workers' practice a unique value.

Service

Social worker's primary goal was and is to help people in need and address social problems. Simply stated, the core value of service and the related goal of helping have been the *sine qua non* of the social work profession. This simplicity, however, can be misleading if the determination concerning whom, how, where, and in what ways one serves and what in fact others experience as helpful are understood clearly. The concept of service to society, on which the superstructure of modern social work rests, was well acknowledged in the religious and moral teachings in India. The spirit of doing good to one's fellow beings, and initiating or taking part in activities for the welfare and common good of all seems to have been special characteristics of Indians in Ancient and Medieval India (Mozumdar, 1971).[13]

Tagore had given utmost emphasis on the aspect of service to mankind. In his essay, *Swadeshi Swamaj* (indigenous society), Tagore had written: "I had said that without wasting time by a futile argument wether the English were our *Raja* (king) or any other was our *Raja*, we should try at first to truly build our country through service and sacrifice". Through his essay 'Society and State', he urged the citizens struggling for independence to serve the society. "Every member of the state must put aside a small voluntary contribution for his country as a matter of daily habit. Additional contributions could be for this nationalist society on festive occasions, such as marriage by way of toll". His own life is a sacrifice for service-from Shilaidaha (presently in Bangladesh) to Sriniketan (in India). He had tried to practice the big ideals he wrote about, both during the period of his management of the family estates as also the Swadeshi Movement. In the 1890s, he was given responsibility to manage the paternal estate on behalf of the Tagore family. For many years he managed the estate with devotion and skill which endeared him to his tenants and gave him recognition from the neighbouring *zamindars* (Landlord) who were tempted to adopt many of the welfare measures introduced by him. For instance, he put apart an amount he received from the Nobel Award to establish an agriculture bank to help the farmers. Up to his last days he was preoccupied with the thought as to how the common man of our country could have a little more food, and better living conditions. He never deceived himself or others with the device of big ideals. On the contrary, he was always on the alert not to allow words to cover up real action (Mahalanobis, 1949:106).[14]

Tagore had emphasized on selfless and non-discriminate service as the motto of his institution. To be true workers in village service, my institution serves the Hindu and the Muslim villagers alike. I do not want anything from villagers in return but only the natural right to serve his fellowmen without any hope of reward. If that spirit could be introduced everywhere in the country their problems would be solved in due course of time.

In his famous novel, *Gora*, one can hear an unmistakable echo of Tagore's own experience in Gora's encounter with villages. In many places it appears he spoke through the voice of his hero and lavishly bestowed on him those qualities–fearlessness, fellow-feeling and an inflexible spirit of service–that are the hallmark of a true servant of the country (Sen, 1991:97).

Dignity and Worth of the Person

Social work rests on the premise of the dignity of human beings. Human beings have intrinsic value. Even if he is born in a family of criminals or brought up in a bad environment, his basic worth is not affected. Even antisocial acts do not deprive the person of his innate dignity, when he indulges in such behaviour, it can be said that he is not acting in conformity with his dignity, but he does not lose his innate dignity thereby. This only proclaims the worth of the individual rather than bestowing it upon him. The idea resonates in Carl Rogers understanding of the intrinsic sense of self.

Respect for the dignity and worth of all people is perhaps the most basic of social work values. However, its application in practice requires a profound commitment to self-determination and strong skills in facilitating the enhancement of self-esteem in others. In promoting the self-determination of the clients, some social workers may possibly confront a sense of dissonance as they weigh their professional knowledge, their professional beliefs, their feelings for their clients against professional standards. Valuing the dignity and worth of each person is a matter of thinking, feeling and acting. Although our respect for the inherent dignity and worth of persons is primarily demonstrated through our professional behaviours, our capacity to behave respectfully is inevitably shaped by our personal experiences and values, professional knowledge and training, openness to feedback from others, and personal and professional commitment to a disciplined use of self.

Looking also at the macro perspective, we can see how Tagore laid emphasis on dignity and worth of an individual. Tagore is the first among our national leaders, (Kabir, 1961:23)[15] to speak of the need of a secular government that paid equal regard to all religions, communities and faith. Tagore believed that wherever the principle of respect for the dignity of groups and individuals has been practiced, the result has been an immense gain for all concerned. Failure to follow this principle has invariably led to impoverishment and ultimate decay of natural culture and prosperity. He held that the only way in which mankind can work out its salvation in the modern world is acceptance of differences among nations in a spirit of mutual respect for each other.

Social Responsibility

The National Association of Social Workers defines social work as, "the professional activity of helping individuals, groups or communities to enhance or restore their capacity for social functioning and creating social conditions favourable to the goal." This could be interpreted to mean that social workers help people to solve life problems so that their lives can be more satisfying and rewarding. If by definition, social workers have a duty to help people solve social problems so that their lives can be more rewarding and satisfying, then the ethical implication is clear. The basic value of social work is the responsibility of social workers to help others achieve a satisfying and rewarding social existence. This moral duty of altruistic social action not only defines but is also put into practice.

The Indian tradition lays emphasis primarily on the concept of duty to one's fellowmen, apparently less to the concept of right. In his relation to the rest of the society, the individual, according to Indian scheme, lays stress upon his duties—*dharma* by which he is to secure his own advancement. Of course, one implies the other, but while right looks to the acquisition of power and comforts for the physical self, the path of duty lies through the discharge of debts which a person owes to all sentient being (Banerjee, 1966).[16]

Tagore unhesitatingly accepted the Western idea of democracy but to this he added the Indian conception of social initiative and social responsibility. He pointed out that in ancient and medieval India, kings had wealth and political power but the richest and the most powerful men were not satisfied till they had received the approbation of their community. This made many of the social welfare activities independent of the power of the state and encouraged initiative and philanthropy among the individual members of society. Tagore insisted that Indians must themselves provide the nation-building services without always looking to the State was derived from his regard for the ancient Indian tradition of social responsibility (Kabir, 1961:19).

Social Justice

Historically since its inception, the social work profession is strongly identified with value of social justice. Challenging injustice and pursuing social change are integral to each professional social worker's duties. When we refer to the concept of 'fairness', justice is often misconstrued to mean equality or altruistic benevolence. However, the concept of justice is much more complicated. In fact, the very concept of justice presupposes selfishness and conflict of interest. If altruistic benevolence prevailed, the concept of justice as right to a balancing of self-interest and conflicts of interests would not be needed. The universally recognized symbol of justice, a blindfold woman holding a balance scale, symbolizes justice as an objective and fair balancing of competing interests.

Also, fairness does not mean always treating people equally. While all people have an equal right to justice, this is not the same as saying that all deserve the same. Fairness sometimes requires treating people differently, for example, if someone works harder than others, justice may argue that they receive the proportionate share of the rewards, rather than an equal share. If someone has been treated unjustly in the past, justice may argue that the proportionate redistribution of resources may be required in the present, rather than an equal distribution. To cite an example, many minorities have not received equal opportunity to participate in the economic institutions of our society. Justice would appear to demand that adequate opportunities be provided to minorities now in proportion to the relevant barriers unjustly sanctioned by our society in the past. Aristotle's definition of justice is still, generally accepted by many as the clearest and most valid. Justice, he said, consist of treating equals equally, and unequally in proportion to their relevant differences.

Social justice can thus be defined as "the embodiment of fairness (whether people are dealt with reasonably), equity (whether similar situations are dealt with equity) and equality (whether people and situations are dealt in the same manner); as an ideal condition in which all members of the society have the same basic rights of protection, opportunities, obligations and social benefits." (Allen-Meares & DeRoos, 1997: 378)[17] Social workers have an ethical responsibility to be informed about the degree to which marginalized communities are ensured equality of opportunity and access to needed information, services, resources and meaningful participation in decision making. Social Workers must use their professional knowledge, skills and influence to enhance equal opportunity and access.

Tagore was a crusader for social justice. Born in a *zamindar* (landlord) family, he turned out to a benevolent landlord. His writings also reflect his conviction towards social justice. An earlier account can be seen in his well-known story called *'Megh-O-Roudra'* (Cloud and Sun) that was written in 1894. While it was essentially a piece of literature, the choice of the theme and the incidents narrated therein reveal the deep impressions of rural life made on his mind (Sen, 1991: 100).[18] Young Sasibhushan, a law graduate living in the village made a determined stand thrice against the wrong doings perpetrated in villages. But his courage was of little avail. Each time he was baffled and in the end had to suffer five years of imprisonment. Indeed it was no easy matter for him to help the victims. The victims would rather tolerate an injustice than fight for its redress. The troubles and expense involved in seeking justice were too much for them. Moreover, they were one and all, afraid to incur the wrath of the ruling class less it should bring upon them a new load of opposition. In another essay, *Raja O Praja* (King and his Subjects) he had vividly illustrated the challenges to ensure social justice. The concluding lines are worth quoting–"How to ensure justice? The very man for whose welfare you would perhaps stake your life, might in his weakness become a source of danger. You could never be sure of receiving the right response from him even to help him. The coward would deny the truth, the persecuted would hide their sufferings, the law would remorselessly raise its iron first while the gates of the prison house would open wide to engulf you (translated by author)."

Another instance is Tagore's famous novel *Gora,* which was begun in 1908, and first published 2 years later. This is about the experience of an urban, educated young man in the villages of Bengal and his efforts to bring about justice. The helplessness of the villagers and their inability to unite even to safeguard their own interests appeared to Gora almost unbelievable. Gora imagined that to overcome evil all that was necessary was to take a firm stand on the side of right. Through Gora, Tagore was expressing the views that under the existing system the dispensation of justice tended to be a one sided affair, the balance being only too often tilted in favour of the strong. Tagore would have been most unhappy to see how in the contemporary democratic system of governance in India political power wins over all the wrong doing and how a corrupt system is established in spite of the provisions of law.

Human Relationship

The profession and the social workers recognize the central importance of human relationships in the practice of social work. The social worker-client relationship is a professional relationship that is positive in nature. Only a positive relationship can serve as a means towards the desirable end of helpfulness from a state of helplessness. The social worker-client relationship has some specific characteristics–it is bound by time and specific purpose; there is an implied authority; it is diffuse in nature and helps in building strong bonds and; it fosters client's growth.

Social workers understand that human development, change and opportunity occur within the context of nurturing, accepting and supportive relationships. Therefore, a central focus of practice with clients is on relationships–bringing honesty into relationships, reducing tension in relationships, redefining or ending relationships when the task is accomplished and developing new relationships for other clients.

In the scheme of rural reconstruction, Tagore emphasized the need to develop rapport with the villagers before the delivery of service. The first step in the strategy of rural reconstruction was not to abruptly approach the villagers with a bundle of schemes for development, but to go slow, that is, to fully understand the nature and extent of the major problems of the village people and to gain their confidence through some urgent welfare actions for them. Until and unless a relation of friendship was established with them as a result of sincere and sympathetic intervention in their life and livelihood, no amount of endeavour to improve their condition and quality of life through their own efforts would bear any fruit (Mukhopadhyay, 1995:5).[19]

'Give with respect' was Tagore's another injunction. This has a two-fold implication for the social worker. There may be a lack of respect in both *what* we give and *how* to give. Quoting the *shastras* he said: '*shradhyeya deyam*–if you give, then give with respect'. To treat villagers with a spirit of condescension and provide for them mere crumbs of culture and education–both are wrong and harmful. Tagore insists on the equality of rights. It is the duty of the rural worker to teach the villagers not to look down upon themselves but to evoke self-confidence among them. This is possible only if there is respect in the interaction. The respect you show to them will breed self-respect and in turn they will learn to respect you. When you have sympathy only then you can truly interact with them, speak their language, feel the beat of their pulse and heart, and ultimately win their sympathy. If you can win this respect and sympathy, more than half the battle for betterment is won. The door of their hearts will open wide and your ideals and ideas of improvement will find an easy entrance.

The principle of respect for the individual and of refusal to impose upon him some system is basic to the approach of Santiniketan and Sriniketan towards education, extension work and to life. The Poet's emphasis on the need for a fundamental respect for and readiness to appreciate the individual, whether they be aboriginal Santal, outcaste Muchi (cobbler) man, woman, boy or girl (Elmhirst, 1939) is the fundamental value towards developing a positive relationship with the people we work with. One should recall that this was during the period where the actions of a number of *bhadra-loks* (Gentlemen) and British Government officials were upsetting and insulting for villagers giving rise to the feeling that they are neither respected nor appreciated as an individual or as a person with their own experience of life.

Self-Help and Mutual-Help

Emerging from the value of innate dignity of beings service is regarded as both self-help and mutual help. The faith in intrinsic motivation is to aspire to live up to one's own dignity. Modern methods of social work emphasizes rightly the need for working with the client, group and community rather than for the client that implies drawing heavily upon the inner resource of people. People are not to be acted upon. The driving principle of cooperative organizations and self-help groups is of self-help and mutual help.

Tagore was a firm believer in cooperation and he saw cooperative endeavour as a viable solution to meet people's needs. He states his ideas of cooperation thus: "it is not enough to say there is a shortage of funds in our country: worse there is shortage of hope. We cast all the blame on fate as we bear torments of hunger. We grovel in the dust, assured that only the mercy of Heaven or of people from outside can save us. It does not strike us that the remedy is in our own hands. That is why it is better to instill hope in the heart than to offer alms. It is his own deficiency, and no decree of fate, that makes a man sink into the depths… Man loses his true stature when he fails to unite fully with his fellows. A complete man is one who has this capacity for union; a lone individual is a fragmented being (Tagore: 323).[20] Tagore strongly felt that the misery of the rural people is both a cause and an effect of their poor condition. He felt that they needed both confidence 'within' themselves and confidence 'without'. Enfeebled, suspicious and dispirited as they were through poverty and exploitation they needed courage and confidence, a spirit of thrift, of self-help and mutual help. There is a natural fear of poverty. It can be encountered if we stand and act as a collective. It is only by combining that man has achieved all that is worthwhile in life-knowledge, faith, power and wealth (*Ibid.*: 324).[21]

Self-help and mutual-help forms the basis for establishing and regularizing the wide variety of cooperative organizations spurred by Sriniketan. It includes cooperative health societies, irrigation societies, grain cooperatives (Dharmagola), agricultural credit cooperatives consumer cooperative stores, weaver's cooperative, etc. "He who is lacking in hope must perish. No one can save him by offering alms or some other help. He must be made to realise that what is not possible for a single individual will be possible when fifty unite in a group and assemble for achievement of a common goal. The fifty who have hitherto cultivated their separate holdings, side by side, will have all the advantages of a large working capital if they pool all their resources–land, labour, granaries" (*Ibid.* : 327).[22] He had hopes in reviving the rural economy of India through cooperation. At one time the cooperative principle was followed to some extent in our village based economy. But life now is not simple as in those days. Besides, it is now far more difficult for the rich to be selfless. So much the better, though; the masses must now develop their own inherent strength–that will be of more permanent worth. If the Indian economy is based once more on cooperation, the villages, which are the nurseries of our civilization, will be vitalized and the whole country will gain a new life (*Ibid.* : 340). Cooperation as an important component of Rural Reconstruction has been dealt with at length in the following chapter.

Integrity

Social workers should aspire to be trustworthy in all professional activities. A high level of integrity implies openness and clarity with the clients or colleagues or even within ourselves. Elaborating on the need of authenticity of the social workers, Mathew (1991)[23] points out the expectation of a certain level of congruence between the private life and the professional life: between what he feels and what he says and between verbal and non-verbal communication, is important. There is no implying, however, that the worker has to communicate his/her feelings at all times. But it implies that the worker does not communicate sentiments contrary to his/her inner-feelings in order to flatter the client or win the client's feelings. If on the other hand, the worker realizes that the feelings are inappropriate as far as the client's welfare is concerned, then the worker may communicate to the client attitudes those that differ from his/her feelings.

If one reads the history of Sriniketan, one can see the background in which Tagore placed his personal experiences of earlier days and his earlier efforts in rural reconstruction at Shilaidaha and Patisar, (now in Bangladesh) put into practice at Sriniketan. In an address to the workers at Sriniketan he said: "Gradually the sorrow and poverty of the villages became clear to me, and I began to grow restless to do something about it. It seemed to me a very shameful thing that I should spend my days as a landlord, concerned only with money-making and engrossed with my own profit and loss. From that time forward, I continually endeavoured to find out how villagers' minds could be aroused, so that they could themselves accept the responsibility for their own lives. If we merely offer them help from outside, it would be harmful to them. How could they themselves be stirred to life? That question gives me much food for thought. It was difficult to help them because they despised themselves." They would say, "we are dogs–only whipping and beating will keep us right". (Tagore, 1908).[24] His own words stress the authenticity of his intervention in rural reconstruction. To inculcate a strong sense of integrity among the workers and villagers, Tagore stressed more on the value system that existed in the past.

Competence

It is the expectation of the profession that professionals should limit their practice to those areas in which they have established a necessary degree of competence. Competence must be established through mastery of the knowledge base about practice, having an exposure to field realities and investing in exploration of one's own values, stereotypes and personal beliefs and biases. Competence is not static, it is dynamic. This implies that the social worker should consciously cultivate the professional expertise, beginning with professional education and continue it for his/her lifetime. It is a process by means of which professional growth and development take place steadily. The growth includes periodic professional renewal, which is a renewal of professional ethos involving expansion of knowledge, sharpening of old techniques, acquiring new techniques and a revitalization of one's commitment. In other words, the social worker is proceeding from 'being' to 'becoming'–'being' from the level of a natural person of automatic responses to 'becoming' a professional person of consciously communicated responses. A beginner in social work starts with a conscious application of techniques, which gradually get transformed into skills through repeated, meaningful doing (Mathew, 1991:190).[25]

The social worker should be an authentic person in terms of possession of warmth and goodwill towards people and a desire to be of help to people in trouble. In some persons, love for people occurs almost like an innate automatic process; nevertheless, what they need is to harness the quality of effective helping of people along scientific lines, there are, on the other hand, persons who admit that they do not have inborn warmth towards people. Nevertheless, they consider helping people as an important activity. Persons belonging to the second group are not unsuitable for social work, provided they are willing to cultivate love for people and other related qualities that are essential for social work. The professional nature of social work signifies that the desirable qualities and techniques required for competent performance of social work can be acquired, and well-motivated persons acquire them by learning and doing (Mathew, 1991: 189).

This is exactly what Tagore said: "Being good social workers presuppose rare qualities of head and heart. It is not enough to be well-wisher; we must know what is good for those whom we wish well. It is not enough to try to serve others; we must acquire the ability to serve. Those who aspire to be servants of the society must, in full consciousness of their mission, qualify themselves for the task. The first essential requisite is to acquire the necessary knowledge and the second is to cultivate the true feelings. One is training of the head and the other is that of heart" (Sen: 1991:124).

Tagore deprecated sentimental or quack remedies. In his 'Call of Truth', he insisted that full information on all relevant points should be collected first in order to decide which economic programme would best meet the needs of the rural population. Rural problems must be tackled with a scientific spirit. Like other economic and social problems, they call for expert handling. That is why he always stressed the necessity of collecting all relevant information on specific issues before suggestions were offered for its solution. 'Knowledge is a necessary prelude to action' and we must know fully the conditions prevailing in the field of work (Tagore in his Pabna address, 1905).

Empowerment

The widespread use of the term 'powerlessness and empowerment' in social work is a relatively recent phenomenon. Since the 1950s, the phenomenon of powerlessness has been examined in social and political science literature and alternatively referred to as alienation, victim-blaming, learned helplessness, internalized oppression or hidden injuries. Powerlessness has increasingly been viewed as an objective phenomenon, where people with little or no political and economic power lack the means to gain greater control and resources in their lives. In its broadest definition, empowerment is a multi-level construct that involves people assuming control and mastery over their lives in the control and purposefulness to exert political power as they participate in the democratic life of their community for social change. It is an ecological construct that applies to interactive change on multiple levels; the individual, organization and community. Community empowerment refers to communities achieving equity of resources, having both equity and capacity to solve problems and solutions, increasing participation in communities, activities leading to improved neighbourhoods, a stronger sense of community and personal and political efficacy and developing a participatory social action model to increase the effectiveness of natural helping systems and supporting practice behaviour for social change (Wallerstein, 1992)[26]. Since the 1930s, Saul Alinsky and his disciples have organized neighbourhoods and community groups through developing 'power' coalitions and confrontational politics. Taken as a whole, empowerment therefore reflects an understanding of the perceived and actual components of powerlessness and encompasses the linkages and interactions between change processes in an individual and organizational community systems. Empowerment becomes the avenue for people to challenge their internalized powerlessness while developing real opportunities to gain control of their own lives and transform their various settings. Alternatively, this can be called processes of participatory self-competence, civic competence, or conscientization and problem-posing from Brazilian educator Paulo Freire. This model includes dimensions of improved self-concept, critical analysis of the world, identification with others as a member of a community, participation with others in organizing for community change, and actual environmental/political change. In sum, empowerment is a social action process that promotes participation of people, organizations and communities towards the goals of increased individual and community control, political efficacy, improved quality of community life and importantly, social justice.

Empowerment is a process that enhances the ability of disadvantaged ('powerless') individuals or groups to challenge and change (in their favour) existing power relationships that place them in subordinate economic, social and political positions. Empowerment can manifest itself in acts of individual resistance, as well as in group mobilization.

Tagore's ideal of empowerment can be seen from a larger perspective of the community and nation building. Tagore's ideal of service is a unique combination of his humanitarianism with individualism and sense of realism. He considered it both unwise and wrong in principle to attempt to do everything for others. No missionary zeal would be enough to serve in this way all the villagers of India. The most dauntless spirit of sacrifice is likely to shrink before the appalling magnitude of the task. He felt that humanitarian services might testify to the nobility of those who serve, but it would keep those who are served in a state of perpetual helplessness and dependence on others. Tagore knew that he could not, as indeed no nation can dispense with the spirit of service, but he never ceased to stress that the best and the real service was that which was directed to awaken the mind and to call forth its latent energies. Tagore said: "I shall not be happy simply to know that the villagers now spins a pound and a half of yarn where he used to spin only one pound or that he now gets a *maund* and a half of paddy where he used to get only a *maund.* I want much more than that. I want a complete awakening of his whole mind," (From an address delivered at the Sriniketan anniversary in February 1940) rouse their minds so that their muscles would be active, he meant to say. If you bear their burden on some occasion, do so; but teach them, above all, to bear their own burden. Serve them by all means, but take care that as a result of your service, they learn to stand on their own feet. The test of your service would lie in the ability of those served to dispense with it. The best way of helping others is to help them to help themselves.

His whole political outlook was consistent with the doctrine that government is best which governs the least. He may have been influenced by the great liberal tradition of the western world when he said that governance should perform the major services for the community. A distinction between the state and the community is inherent in Tagore's thought. He believed that progress lies in circumscribing the functions of the State and transferring them to the community. He was thus a strong supporter of local self-government in every sphere of life. The individual finds fulfilment only when he is autonomous. The community also flourishes when it is responsible for its own welfare. He was therefore, for decentralization of authority and held that the State should deal only with those aspects of social life that cannot be administered by the individual or the group. In a word, his conception of politics was essentially that of a decentralized and federative state in which local units would increasingly play a role (Kabir: 1961: 18-19).[27]

When individuals become self-reliant and develop knowledge, moral purposes and aesthetic perception, India would forthwith become free. One can see this idea being expressed in his presidential address of call to work for economic self-sufficiency and social freedom.

In the foregoing discussion we have tried to find roots for some of the core social work values in Tagorean thoughts and ideals of rural reconstruction that evolved out of his educational philosophy based on utilitarian principles. According to this, education that is devoid of human needs have no meaning. Education should cater towards human growth and development. Analogous to this is that if growth and development should transpire, it should preclude education and conscientization. Nine core values of the profession–service, dignity and worth of individuals, social responsibility, social justice, importance of human relationship, self-help, integrity, competence and empowerment have been discussed in the light of the social philosophy of Tagore. Even though they are discussed as distinct items, the discussion itself shows the interconnectedness between the different values. From the practice point of view, one can say that the value of services to others is the most important one. The other values mentioned above characterize the quality of service offered and hence if the service has to be effective and efficient, a conviction of the other values is a must. The modern social work profession in India and abroad have followed the values and principles which were applied by Tagore from the beginning of the 20th century that were born out of his observations and perceptions developed during his visit to the communities. The sufferings of the people in social, economic and heath related issues moved him to take up interventions from 1905 and finally launching the project–the Sriniketan Experiment with Leonard Knight Elmhirst as the Director in 1922. The project is till date based in the Sriniketan campus of Visva-Bharati University and caters its services to more than fifty communities. Of late, it has been decided to cover more than 100 communities with similar need-based services as a social responsibility of the university and to create a practice laboratory for the learners and practitioners of agriculture, social work, cottage industry and rural management. Research and innovation will be the key components for the academic and practicing professionals in its efforts in rural reconstruction by creating model communities. This forms the core focus what can be called the 'rural incubation centre'.

BIBLIOGRAPHICAL REFERENCE

Allen-Meares, P. & Y. DeRoos: 'The Future of Social Work Profession' in Michael R. & Eileen G. (ed.): *Social Work in the 21st Century,* Pine Forge Press, California, 1997.

Amir Ali Hashim: 'Rural Research in Tagore's Sriniketan', *The Modern Review, Vol. 56(91),* 1934.

Banerjee, Gauri Rani: *Papers on Social Work–An Indian Perspective, TISS Series No. 23,* Tata Institute of Social Sciences, 1075: 'Concepts of Social Work in the Gita', *Indian Journal of Social Work,* Vol. 25 (1), 1964.

Benerjee, Hiranmay: *Experiments in Rural Reconstruction,* Visva-Bharati, Calcutta, 1966.

Biswas, K. and S. Sengupta: *Rural survey–Ballavpur, pre census Population Studies Institute,* Indian Statistical Institute, Calcutta, 1975.

Chatterjee Rai Bahadur Sukumar: 'The Cooperative Health Societies under Visva Bharati', *The Modern Review,* Vol. 67, 1940.

'Sriniketan 1921-1941–A Bibliographical Introduction', *Visva Bharati Journal of Research, Humanities and Social Sciences,* Vol. 4(1), 1980.

Dasgupta, Sugata: *Poet and a Plan–Tagore's Experiments in Rural Reconstruction,* Thacker Spink & Co. Pvt. Ltd., Calcutta, 1962.

Voluntary Organisations in Rural Development–A Global Model, Social Policy and Peace Series, Society for Developing Gramdans, New Delhi, 1973.

Elmhirst, L.K: 'An Experiment in Rural Reconstruction'. *The Modern Review*, Vol. 33 (4), 1923.

'Our Work at Sriniketan', *Visva-Bharati News*, January 1939.

'Rebuilding the Villages', in the *Centenary Book on Tagore*, Calcutta, 1961.

Poet and Ploughman, Visva-Bharati, Calcutta, 1975.

Frederic, G. Reamer: 'Ethical Issues for Social Work Practice' in Michael R. & Eileen G. (eds.): *Social Work in the 21st Century*, Pine Forge Press, California, 1997.

Ghosh, Amiya Kumar & Banerjee Tarasankar: *Brati-Balak Sangha and National movement in Birbhum*, 1990.

Gordon, W.E.: 'Knowledge and Value–Their Distinction and Relationship in Clarifying Social Work Practice', *Social Work*, Vol. 10 (3), 1965.

Joseph, Sherry (ed.): *Social Work in the Third Millennium–Some Concerns and Challenges*, Department of Social Work, Visva-Bharati, Sriniketan, 2000.

Kabir, Humayan: 'Introduction', in *Rabindranath Tagore: Towards Universal Man*, Asia Publishing House, Bombay, 1961.

Mahalanobis, P.C.: 'Rabindranath Tagore', *Visva-Bharati Quarterly*, Vol. 15 (2), 1949.

Mathew, Grace: *An Introduction to Social Case Work*, Tata Institute of Social Sciences, Bombay, 1992.

Mozumdar, S.N.: *Community Development in India*, Visva-Bharati, 1971.

NASW: Code of Ethics of the National Association of Social Workers, National Association of Social Workers, USA, 1996.

Ray, Benoy Gopal: 'Rabindranath on Values', in Bhattacharya K. (ed): *Rabindranath Tagore Birth Centenary Celebrations, Proceedings of Conferences, Vol. III, (Indian Philosophical Congress, 36th Session)*, Visva-Bharati, 1961.

Sinha, Dikshit: 'Tagore Experiment in Health Care–Health and Medicine as an Aid to Rural Reconstruction', in Sen, Suchibrata (ed): *Health and Environment in Late Colonial Period of Bengal*, 2002.

Sen, Sudhir: *Rabindranath Tagore on Rural Reconstruction*, Visva-Bharati Economic Research Publication, No. 2, 1943, reprint 1991.

Tagore, Rabindranath: *The Religion of Man*, Visva-Bharati, Publication Division, Calcutta, 2000: 'Objectives of Palli Samaj', *Palliprakriti*, Visva-Bharati, Calcutta, 1908.

Timbres, Harry: *Report of Medical Condition in Birbhum District*, Visva-Bharati Quarterly, Vol. 7(3), 1930.

TISS: Declaration of Ethics for Professional Social Workers, Tata Institute of Social Sciences, 1977 (Pamphlet).

'Rabindranath on National Reconstruction', *The Modern Review*, Vol. 39 (5), 1926, p. 706.

Wadia, A.R.: *History and Philosophy of Social Work in India*, Allied Publishers Pvt. Ltd., Bombay, 1961.

Wallerstein, Nina: 'Powerlessness, Empowerment and Health: Implications for Health Promotion Programme', *American Journal of Health Promotion*, Vol. 6 (3), 1992.

NOTES

1. The author acknowledge Sherry Joseph's participation in this chapter.
2. https://www.ifsw.org/what-is-social-work/global-definition-of-social-work/
3. Banerjee, Gauri Rani*: Papers on Social Work–An Indian Perspective, TISS Series No. 23,* Tata Institute of Social Sciences, 1075. 'Concepts of Social Work in the Gita', *Indian Journal of Social Work,* Vol. 25 (1), 1964.
4. Wadia, A.R.*: History and Philosophy of Social Work in India,* Allied Publishers Pvt. Ltd., Bombay, 1961.
5. Sen Sudhir: *Rabindranath Tagore on Rural Reconstruction,* Visva-Bharati Economic Research Publication, No. 2, 1943, reprints 1991.
6. Dasgupta, Sugata*: Poet and a Plan–Tagore's Experiments in Rural Reconstruction,* Thacker Spink & Co. Pvt. Ltd., Calcutta, 1962.
7. *Ibid.*; 35.
8. *Tagore Rabindranath: The Religion of Man*, Visva-Bharati, Publication Division, Calcutta, 2000: 'Objectives of Palli Samaj', Palliprakriti, Visva-Bharati, Calcutta, 1908.
9. Kabir, Humayan: 'Introduction', in *Rabindranath Tagore: Towards Universal Man,* Asia Publishing House, Bombay, 1961.
10. Ray, Benoy Gopal: 'Rabindranath on Values', in Bhattacharya K. (ed.): *Rabindranath Tagore Birth Centenary Celebrations, Proceedings of Conferences, Vol. III, (Indian Philosophical Congress, 36th Session),* Visva-Bharati, 1961.
11. Frederic G Reamer: 'Ethical Issues for Social Work Practice' in Michael R. & Eileen G. (eds.): *Social Work in the 21st Century*, Pine Forge Press, California, 1997.
12. *NASW: Code of Ethics of the National Association of Social Workers,* National Association of Social Workers, USA, 1996.
13. Mozumdar S.N.: *Community Development in India,* Visva-Bharati, 1971.
14. Mahalanobis, P.C.: 'Rabindranath Tagore', *Visva-Bharati Quarterly,* Vol. 15(2), 1949.
15. Kabir, Humayan: 'Introduction', in *Rabindranath Tagore: Towards Universal Man,* Asia Publishing House, Bombay, 1961.
16. Benerjee, Hiranmay: *Experiments in Rural Reconstruction,* Visva-Bharati, Calcutta, 1966.
17. Allen-Meares P. & Y. DeRoos:'The Future of Social Work Profession' in Michael R. & Eileen G. (ed.): *Social Work in the 21st Century,* Pine Forge Press, California, 1997.
18. Sen, Sudhir, 'Rabindranath Tagore on Rural Reconstruction', Visva-Bharati Economic Research Publication, Visva-Bharati, Calcutta, 1991.
19. Mukhopadhyay, Arun: 'Tagore's Sriniketan Experiment–Past and the Present: An Assessment', *IASSI Quarterly*, Vol. 13 (4), 1995.

20. Tagore, Rabindranath, 'The Religion of Man', Visva-Bharati Publication, Reprint 2000, Calcutta.
21. *Ibid.*
22. *Ibid.*
23. Mathew, Grace: *An Introduction to Social Case Work,* Tata Institute of Social Sciences, Bombay, 1992.
24. 'Rabindranath on National Reconstruction', *The Modern Review*, Vol. 39(5), 1926.
25. Mathew Grace: *An Introduction to Social Case Work,* Tata Institute of Social Sciences, Bombay, 1992.
26. Wallerstein Nina: *'Powerlessness, Empowerment and Health: Implications for Health Promotion Program', American Journal of Health Promotion*, Vol. 6(3), 1992.
27. Kabir, Humayan: 'Introduction', in *Rabindranath Tagore: Towards Universal Man,* Asia Publishing House, Bombay, 1961.

4

Tagore's Cooperative Movement

An Initiative in Community Social Work

In one of the poems in The *Gitanjali* (Song Offerings), Tagore wrote, "my heart can never find its way to where thou keepest company with the companionless among the poorest, the lowliest and the lost."[1]

Tagore's cooperative movement was not only an endeavour to fight against poverty and exploitation of the poor by the powerful but also a broad based welfare approach to inculcate the impetus for collective action in mitigating socio-economic problems vulnerable people encounter in their life. It shows a humanitarian approach to holistic development with collective ownership of assets and liabilities for the greater common purpose so that development is sustainable and holistic. He wrote, "humanity is composed of individuals, yet they have their interconnection with human relationship, which gives solidarity to man's world. The entire universe is linked with us in similar manner, it is a human universe."[2] Human relationships in social work, is the core principle of practice without which the desired goal cannot be achieved. Cooperative is that platform for developing human relationships and it is possible to apply to human welfare through collective efforts of the members of the organization. Tagore started establishing various cooperative organizations for community welfare and development at the turn of the 20th century when community social work as a core method of social work discipline was not even coined. A few sporadic attempts in other parts of the world were being made in the form of Settlement House Movements in UK (Toynbee Hall Movement, London 1884) and USA (Hull House Movement, Chicago, 1889). These attempts at community development were city and slum based interventions for migrant industrial workers aimed at the improvement of their quality of life in industrial slums. This chapter attempts to review Tagore's cooperative principles and cooperative organizations with reference to community social work or community organization as one of the primary methods of social work practice that emerged almost simultaneously at the turn of the 20th century. It is indeed remarkable that the progressive ideas of Social Work methods evolved through the movements of Tagore in rural Bengal and the urban slum initiatives of Toynbee and few others. This is not commonly acknowledged in international writings as Tagore's contribution is little known outside the vernacular. This volume is an endeavour to make known the cognitive deliberations of Tagore recognised more as poet than a doer. This fact has not been highlighted as yet in Social Work literature though it is significant in understanding the evolution and modernization of an academic discipline. The question, whether growth or decline of cooperative business is impacting the economic power of large corporations and non-profit business and improving the quality of human lives needs exploration. To Tagore, this question had a definite answer. As a social philosopher, he initiated the organizations of self-sufficient institutions in the form of cooperatives that were built on the capital of people's strengths for their own benefit. In other words, Tagore was a firm believer in collective efforts and the dynamics of collective strength. All through his life, especially from the moment he came in contact with rural life intimately from 1890 onwards, he was deeply pained by the suffering of the rural folk, over which the poor had very little control and blamed their ill fate without realizing that something could be done to offset their condition. Tagore observed that the poor and vulnerable people depend on moneylenders for borrowing at an exorbitant rate of interest calculated and collected every month. He wanted liberation of the poor from such indebtedness by building their own cooperative banks at the community level. He opened the first cooperative credit bank in 1905 at Patisar (now in Bangladesh) where he donated funds to begin the service of creating a credit cooperative for lending and recovery at the grass-root level with minimum interest for the maintenance and growth of the organization. In the later years, he deposited a large part of his Nobel Prize money in the bank. While Tagore applied the savings and credits at macro level through cooperatives through his Experiment in Rural Reconstruction; Professor Muhammad Yunus more than fifty years later through Grameen Bank (1983) in Bangladesh used the similar concept as micro credit to empower the rural poor. Dr. Yunus successfully implemented the concept of Self Help Groups, a more contemporary model of bottoms-up approach for the uplift of the underprivileged. Amul was founded in 1946 at Anand in Gujarat with a mission to strengthen the milk producers.

Amul is managed by the Gujarat Co-operative Milk Marketing Federation Ltd. (GCMMF), which is jointly owned by more than 3.6 million milk producers of Gujarat.[3] Amul in India which is now a multinational corporate body of milk cooperative that has flourished and spread to states and in the nation very fast because of the leadership and its professional management.

A century ago Tagore had envisaged that "when one man, or a group of people, aided by some opportunity, captures the means and material of power"[4] (Tagore, 1929: 36) the 'other' becomes powerless. Cooperative movement makes people powerful with the resources and funds they accumulate for their own use as social business. The capital for the poor is their labour, a conjoined power of many people and that can be shaped into wealth. If they say "we will combine our strength" their real capital will be in their own hands. The oppressed must say to themselves, "It is our divided strength, concentrated in the hands of the mighty, which has given them power. By attacking power we can break it but we cannot put it together again, and so it will be no good to us. We must, therefore, try to combine all our labour power and thereby gain economic benefits to be shared by all"[5]

(Tagore 1929: 37). The rift between the mighty and the weak in the world of materials affairs is the most serious danger today.

With this conviction Tagore laid stress on organization of credit cooperatives, health cooperatives, consumers' cooperatives, farmer's cooperatives etc., in his experiment of rural reconstruction at Sriniketan. He wanted to educate people and unite them for their own causes, i.e. fighting poverty, ill health and ignorance. The inherent principles of cooperative were envisaged to usher in self-reliance to fulfil the basic needs of the poor and vulnerable people. To quote Tagore, "the cooperative principle is progressing in European countries, which have an advantage over us–they have more experience and sense of combination. We Indians are ......backward in this respect. But it may well be expected that even we, goaded by our unbearable poverty and by our great longing for a better life, will ultimately accept the cooperative way. If we fail, there will be no escape from our woes and no one can be blamed on that score"[6] (*ibid.*: 38). The educational and other life experiences of the people of those countries are not similar to our country, therefore, he considered backwardness on our part but he strongly believed that there are ways to train and educate these vulnerable sections of the society through development and cooperation.

The International Cooperative Alliance defines cooperative as "an autonomous association of persons united voluntarily to meet their common economic, social, and cultural needs and aspirations through a jointly owned and democratically controlled enterprise."[7] In India, registration and compliance with the law of the land has demoted the cooperative organization. Autonomy in the cooperative organization though talked about but hardly practiced because of which common people find it cumbersome to comply with these laws. This is a major setback for cooperative institutions to grow or function in the country.

Tagore believed that the systems of societies in which needs were limited to the local level, collective efforts would reap rich dividends. He also envisaged that for cooperatives to be successful there is need for a shift in goals–economic relations within a community changing from primacy of profits to primacy of services and evolution of values governing personal and collective actions, only then we will be able to foster cooperative community life. He was convinced that if we can bring back a semblance of the patterns of a culture where needs of the people were limited, life could be governed with values governing personal and collective conduct geared to greater good. There are instances of successful organisation that operate involving local people and local resources. The Amar Kutir Society for Rural Development is one such example. It can be seen how this organisation has grown and shaped itself over the years by maintaining Tagorean principles of cooperative and Gandhiji's principles of ethical business.[8]

It has been ideally said that poverty will be rooted out if our living is reduced to simple necessities, as it was in the imagined past. This is impracticable in the modern era as change is constant and no human society has ever retraced it footsteps. Human intelligence has to express itself in newer creations through the ages. At one time, the cooperative principle was followed to some extent in our village based economy; however, they were expressed more in cooperation within the community rather than a democratically structured collective service delivery system based on expressed/statutory principles and sharing of responsibility. Tagore too, had observed these with which the poor often relegated the responsibility of their own lives to the hands of the rich or the powerful assuming that they lacked in individual agencies. But life was not as simple as those days (Tagore; 1929). In spite of all, Tagore firmly believed that if cooperative principles were nourished our civilization would be vitalized and the whole country would gain a new life. Tagore gives us the hope that this country can be rescued from age-old poverty by applying cooperative principles in all the economic and social systems that govern the social order as has been proved in our own country time and again through some of the well-functioning cooperatives.

Another self-affirming movement is the Self Employed Women's Association (SEWA), a trade union registered in 1972. It is an organization of poor, self-employed women workers. These are women who earn a living through their own labour or small businesses. They do not obtain regular salaried employment with welfare benefits like workers in the organized sector. They are the unprotected labour force of our country. These are workers of the unorganized sector constituting 93 per cent of the total workforce. However, their work is counted as unpaid service and hence remains invisible. In fact, women workers themselves remain uncounted, undercounted and invisible.[9] It consists of 84 Cooperatives with 11,610 members, a majority of them are successful crafts based cooperatives organizing the artisans and marketing their products supporting the livelihood of thousands of people involving women folk of western India. SEWA at present is a movement which has few hundred thousand active women members across the Indian states.

Training and Development of Human Resources at the Community Level

In implementing the unique and innovative efforts of Tagore to develop desired human resources needed for the future, he organized training and education for rural people right from their childhood to make them disciplined and productive. The daily system of physical workouts was as part of education itself unknown in the villages of Bengal as people believed that since their way of life involved manual effort, they were not in need of organized and systematic exercise. This regularity of exercise fostered certain principles like, bonding between members, emergence of leadership, obedience, participation, and discipline along with the cultivation of physical strength and health. Adolescent boys and girls were formed into groups who went round from home to home collecting first-hand reports of the conditions of families in the village so that timely help and assistance could be provided. Young men formed clubs where they could assemble and plan their assignments. These sessions not only provided engagement to the youth in constructive work but also gave them a purpose and feeling of solidarity towards their own community. They took up activities like community cleaning, responding promptly and effectively to events like fire, illness, disaster, security that made the villagers rely on the youth. Many years later, these activities came to be recognized as extension of service and a necessary component of education. A few of the Indian universities and educational institutions have incorporated extension work in their curriculum modules that impart extension of education to community; Visva-Bharati is unique in designing an entire campus and a clutch of courses built round village extension both as practice as well as pursuing it as an academic discipline. Tagore modelled his *Brati dal* on the Scout movement that started in the villages around Sriniketan. In the words of Tagore, "these *Bratis* are not rich, not educated, but volunteers to country. They are ready to eradicate poverty, sufferings and unhappiness. They want to win the country by winning the hearts of the people who are exploited, vulnerable, and are in danger. It is also found across the world that there are such people but there are few to eradicate the sufferings of those that suffer. They are dedicated to remove the sufferings of the poor and vulnerable."[10] Organizing the youth for delivering services at the community level is a unique kind of cooperation with the motto 'service to mankind'.

Rural Organization for Rural Reconstruction on Cooperative Model

Cooperation was core to Tagore's philosophy of Rural Reconstruction that has been given rather short shrift in academics. "Rabindranath's writings on cooperation and cooperatives were stretched over a period, 1891-1929."[11] Cooperation among the people in society is not usually seen as essential for living in a consumerist world; but the notion of cooperation and its need for social satisfaction of living together is still relevant for human happiness. The business model that has gained currency in the world is profit-driven and not people-centric. Tagore did not create structures for big and large businesses rather he focused on small-scale cottage industries through which cooperatives of artisans and their skills could be brought under meaningful and beneficial structures and process. One such model is thriving in Sriniketan area founded with inspiration from Tagore.

Amar Kutir Society for Rural Development has set a benchmark of not only upholding Tagorean principles but also earning profit for its members through self-management systems and its ability to transfer ownership of organization to the members who are actively engaged in the task of production, design and sales of handicrafts. Furthermore, promotion of cooperative business organization in the interest of the people is welcome as it gives them ownership of organizations for the service to people with additional amount of dividend from the business. The cooperative model of business organizations provide fair price to the producers and the consumers eliminating the layers of middlemen who actually soak up a chunk of the proceeds depriving the producers and consumers. If Amul Cooperative benefiting the milk producers can achieve the status of a multi-national corporate there is scope for other cooperatives initiated at the grassroots involving the rural masses also meeting the local, national and international demands. However, we need to keep in mind that Tagore did not work with large structures; he concentrated on small village communities who could be trained to hone their skills in the crafts and artisanship as well as work together for common aims and goals. He was conscious that the skills in crafts could not morph into large conglomerates but that several crafts coming together could have a better market especially when the artisans are provided training in developing designs and maintaining production standards. These were the goals of Silpa Sadana, the Department of Crafts and Design that started from the very early days of Sriniketan work in 1922. In fact, even in the decade after Tagore's death, his son, Rahindranath and his wife Pratima took the products of Silpa Sadana to national attention and it sustained itself with the profits generated through sales and the demand created in the market.

Social entrepreneurship is an alternative to empowerment of rural communities with their products reaching the consumers as other corporate like Tata, Reliance, Birla are doing. Tagore set us on the path and we can always try with innovation and entrepreneurship to develop such models that will be people-friendly and oriented towards the achievement of common goals of health and happiness and maintain a decent quality of life.

Models of Cooperatives for Holistic Development

Granary or the grain stores were organized from 1927 in each community of the command area of Sriniketan for storing the food grains during the harvest and distribution among the members for consumption during the slack season. It is also a unique cooperation advocated and implemented in Sriniketan Experiment. Many villages had grain silos or structures like towers in which harvested grain was stored; records of deposits were kept and that was regarded as the credit to be drawn upon during times of need. It is important to remember that in the areas where Tagore actively implemented the Sriniketan Experiment, cultivation depended entirely upon the monsoon resulting in single crop in a year. Hence, there used to be a lean period during which there was practically no income. The farmers could then draw upon their accumulated grain to tide over the lean periods. This system of granary cooperatives eliminated the crop lenders who normally charged interest @ 1=1.5 against lending period of six months duration. The granary organized at the community eliminated the exploitation of the grain lenders and the landlords. This led to capacity building of the villagers for their own cause.

Credit Cooperative for Farmers later on named Agricultural Banks was another dream project of Tagore to stop exploitation of poor farmers against moneylenders with high rate of interest. Tagore carried out the management of the ancestral properties or estates situated now in Bangladesh starting from 1890. As has already been mentioned in Chapter 3, the credit society for the farmers was first established in 1905 at Patisar, to stop exploitation of farming communities who had to borrow from the moneylenders at high rate of interest dictated by the providers and remain in debt until death. As early as 1915 Tagore donated a part of his Nobel Prize money to the cooperative bank in order to keep it afloat. The same principles were applied in the Sriniketan experiment. It was common to obtain credit or loan in times of need from feudal lords of the locality or money-lenders who mostly came from Afghanistan known as Kabuliwallas. Tagore, through cooperatives tried to address the issues arising out of unscrupulous usury. The other aspect that Tagore intervened was to seek expertise that would increase agricultural production through use of technology and irrigation. A model agricultural farm was set up; a windmill purchased, transported and set up; newer techniques were demonstrated; soil testing was started but somehow the farmers did not respond favourably. It must be admitted that not enough time was given for such changes to set in, given the fact of history and tradition of practices. However, to help farmers in availing resources for farming he could successfully establish credit cooperatives and cooperative banks in the area of experiment. In the year 1932, there were 222 cooperatives working in the command area (Visva-Bharati Annual Report, 1933). These cooperatives were organized, monitored and supported by Visva-Bharati Cooperative Bank as the Apex Bank. In one of the review meetings held in 1934 Tagore said, "unless the bank shows more enterprise in helping to organize and advance money to various types of cooperative societies and if it sticks to its programme of lending money to credit societies only, I am afraid there is not much justification for members taking part in it." It was therefore, resolved that "they should engage one special officer of Supervisor grade for our Sriniketan area only whose function would be to promote rural cooperative societies of various types as experiments in rural development. Those that are successful could then serve as models for the whole bank area."[12] However, a few cooperatives continued to support the farmers for more than five decades, i.e. till 1980s but closed after the banks were nationalized and government introduced subsidies to farmers. Incidentally, the Visva-Bharati Cooperative Bank established in 1928 is still functioning though the aims and objectives have greatly altered as has the membership that is now restricted only to the employees and ex-employees of the university. The major causes for failure of the cooperatives established during Tagore's time were the paucity of capital as many members defaulted in paying back the loan. From the beginning of the five-year-plans, the government launched a variety of schemes to meet the needs of the farmers and on occasions, loans taken by farmers were waived citing bad monsoon, natural calamities or crop failure. During the early days of independence, Indian economy was largely agricultural and this was seen as the primary sector. Over time, agriculture has lost its primacy in contributing to the national economy.

Health Cooperatives (1932)

During the colonial period, India was the country where 40 per cent children faced death before the age of 5 years, about 50 per cent of the youth could survive up to the age of 20 years and only 15 per cent of the population could live up to the age of 60 years.[13] Main causes of such deaths were malaria, cholera, tuberculosis, plague, fever, small pox, hunger leading to anaemia and many other unknown diseases. Tagore also observed that poor hygienic habits and lack of knowledge among the masses were responsible for illness and death. Treatment against disease was only *ayurvedic* (naturopathy) as modern treatment was partly available only in cities that could be afforded by the rich and elite. In fact, India was then a disease-ridden and death-driven country. At one point of time in 1921, the death rate in the project area (Birbhum District) was 46 per cent against the birth rate of 34 per cent. Tagore, as mentioned earlier, was moved by the state of treatment of the sick, ignorant and helpless rural people who were his subjects who did nothing but blamed their fate as the cause of their suffering. In an address inviting cooperation on malaria control and prevention in 1924, he said "how many births and deaths are taking place, what is the number of people increasing/adding every year is not a big issue; if those who are surviving, are living as human beings is the concern. Their activity, use of intellect is a major issue....physical weakness generates mental weakness... those who survive with mere subsistence, who have no excess, does not lead a human life in the true sense, if life is not active; there cannot be creation in civilization. Where there is misery of life; there will be selfishness"[14]

When Tagore proposed the concept of health cooperative, the rural folk of a cluster of villages had responded very positively towards its organization and management. The health cooperatives used to hire a doctor, one pharmacist and one attendant for its functioning. The families had to subscribe a meager amount per person per annum for availing the health services which included doctors' consultation fees, and some medicines. This unique method of health care for the rural folk continued to serve people in the command area up to 1970s until the state took over the health services on a massive scale in all the districts. One of the health cooperative at Surul village still operates and provides service to its members.

He was of the opinion that if the quality of life is not complete in all respects, the materialistic life will bring further sufferings, be it health, education, economic, or happiness in life. Between 1932 and 1939, there were 8 health cooperatives established in different communities covering about 68 villages in Birbhum district.[15] Most of the patients being treated in these health centres were suffering from malaria or cholera infected through mosquito bites and drinking water respectively. The colonial government did not care about the health issues of the people at any point of time. Health of the people in communities needed care and support as there were no services available in or around the communities except those areas where some missionaries were organizing health services especially during the break out of epidemics.

Since the state has taken over all the matters related to health services for its citizens, the need for organizing health cooperatives with the people, by the people and for the people is no longer necessary. However, it is difficult to explain the rapid growth of private health services even in rural areas when the government has seemingly taken health care system under its ambit of administration and service delivery to the people. The reasons are probably related to the increasing economic strength of rural people; their lack of confidence in the state health service systems and the quality of the state run hospital facilities. Health cooperatives would not have been able to afford the services of reputed medical practitioners or afford the rising cost of allopathic drugs. The entry of the insurance companies providing health coverage is another factor that has eroded the base of health cooperatives as well as making private medical services like hospitalization not only available but affordable to a certain extent. The government too in trying to keep pace with changing demands of people and their aspirations for enhanced services has launched health schemes with in-built insurance for all sections of the population with especial focus on the populations that lie below the poverty line. The sustainability of quality health services, whether through state or private service providers is questioned now and then. Tagore's advocacy for participatory health management system taking the beneficiaries as one of the stakeholders seems more sustainable today. Rural society today is totally different from what it was a century ago but the thoughts and approach of rural development envisaged by Tagore are still relevant.

Cooperative Banks

A collectively developed and managed financial organization in rural society was non-existent when Tagore thought of cooperative bank at the community level for the benefit of the poor and vulnerable people, mostly subjected to exploitations by the landlords and moneylenders. As per the Visva-Bharati annual reports, the credit cooperative societies (Cooperative Banks) at and around Sriniketan were established from 1926 onwards.[16] These cooperative societies attempted to alleviate poverty and to free the poor from borrowing from moneylenders at high rate of interest. The members of the cooperative banks borrowing from their own organization were charged 12.5 per cent interest annually. Furthermore, the capital of the cooperatives was subscribed by the members which is the strength of the organization and the members. Later on, to facilitate the administration of the cooperatives an apex cooperative bank was established at Santiniketan to monitor and support the activities of the cooperative banks at the community level. The concept of Self Help Groups and micro finance probably emerged from this concept of cooperative banks which is a macro level intervention of similar nature. Social work intervention with its focus on empowerment of the people, considers this as a viable means of economic empowerment for social development.

Consumer's Cooperative

Villagers buy their daily consumables from the shop run by pretty business people at a price quoted by the traders. The traders make a profit unknown to the consumers. Tagore wanted the stores to be owned by the consumers themselves so that the profit comes back to them which could be another source of income. He organised a number of consumers' cooperative with the help of community leaders. One such consumer's cooperative store meant for the employees of his institution still serves the employees and a sizeable number of people in locality. During the late 1970s and 1980s, the consumers' cooperatives were the backbone of the village economy in the communities adopted by Visva-Bharati University. Consumers' cooperatives were also built with members' contribution and management making it as a fair price shop open to all who wish to buy commodities sold at the stores. The members were eligible to share the profit earned at the end of every accounting year. These organizations at the community level gave the poor an opportunity of ownership and management for their own benefit and economic empowerment. Interestingly, the Visva-Bharati Cooperative Society still runs its own departmental store and its management is based on the cooperative principles and cooperative act.

Weaver's Cooperative

The weaver's conditions of life were no better than what it is today. In fact, Mahatma Gandhi did give a call for indigenous means of weaving cloth but this could not compete with mill products. This made handloom cloth more expensive and the weavers were left without a market.

The quality of life of the weavers was then deplorable. He made an all out effort to organize the weavers through weavers' cooperatives and bargain for fair price of their products. He was in favour of using technology that could be afforded by the organization of cooperatives of the weavers. These cooperatives were collectives that could negotiate to protect their interests right from purchasing of machines, raw materials, price of the products. In other words, Tagore wanted to organize the weavers to protect their interest collectively. These cooperatives were built by members' effort and managed by themselves in a democratic manner. The weavers are not simply producer but stakeholders in the society and organizations. This can also be termed as trade based empowerment for vulnerable weavers.

Labour Bank

The working classes in rural communities who lived hand to mouth needed to protect their interest and save some of their income for the hard times when they will not have employment. The main objectives of forming Labour Cooperative was to stop bonded labour and empower them to bargain for their legitimate claims like minimum and fair wages against the work performed by them. His basic approach in organizing all cooperatives comprised of mobilizing, organizing, empowering the members to protect their interest and live a life free from hazards and uncertainty. All labour could join this organization as a member and pay the subscription for obtaining loan and could return the capital through regular instalments. As done in other cooperatives here too he laid stress on capacity building and empowerment approach for intervention with the working class.

Community Social Work Practice and Its Relevance to Cooperative Society

Reviewing the philosophy, approaches and principles Tagore applied in organizing cooperatives at the community level, let us explore how social work profession can contribute towards the empowerment of rural poor applying similar principles matching the contexts/

situation and needs of the individual, groups and the society at large. Tagore organized all types of cooperatives at the community level to eliminate exploitation and discrimination of the powerful having access to resources at their disposal. The present scenario is not much different from those days except the nature and means of exploitation is sophisticated under different names and forms. The poor still remains unorganized and helpless in all aspects of their lives. They live hand to mouth and are born with debts and die in debts. The government policy, projects, schemes have failed to reach the goals set since last 75 years in free India. The people in power holding positions in administration are acquiring wealth and enhancing the distance between the rich and the poor.

Social work since its inception has been addressing poverty and ill health. Many a people in India today live in extreme poverty, illiteracy, ignorance, and especially in rural areas many suffer from preventable diseases including malnutrition which indicates the nature of socio-economic condition of the people in general. Access to finance and organizations with ownership is the only available options for empowerment and development of the poor. Cooperative societies can be organized at all the levels of economic transactions of the society. Social workers need to work on it by nurturing the self help groups into a cluster in the form of cooperative societies making social entrepreneurs active in the organization and management of these organizations built on people's strengths. To achieve the goal, we need to educate the groups and their leaders on organization and management of small-scale organizations with affiliation to large organizations–an umbrella for promotion and protection of people's cooperative societies. Tagore was of the opinion that universities shall spread its learning centres in the communities for practical and vocational education. The time has come when we need to develop a curriculum for the poor to learn household credit and management of domestic economy at the family level and small organizations for production and marketing at the community level.

Social work profession lays stress on bringing in change in attitude and behaviour, knowledge and skills, and practice of the people for developing the quality of life; hence behaviour-change models need to be developed. The people in modern society are self-centric; hence forming cooperative society needs a tremendous change in their mindset–feeling of togetherness for a common cause in the larger interest of all the members of the society. Whereas the poor lack in knowledge and skills, the primary focus should be on these two aspects, i.e. knowledge for developing cooperative societies and skills for managing and maintaining the organizations. Once the attitude, knowledge and skills are developed, behaviour and practice will lead to a trend for cooperation. To make it happen social workers will have to convince the mass that their conditions of life will change following an exercise of re-shaping their knowledge and skills in development and management of organizations. At the first instance, the change leaders from and within the community should be targeted for training and education. Educated and unemployed youths of the community will be the best leaders if nurtured with required skills. The boy and girl scouts can be taken into confidence and be trained to be social entrepreneurs for the purpose.

Need Identification

The rural communities are mainly dependent on farming and allied trades like dairy, poultry, goat and sheep rearing, etc. The main problem they face is in marketing the products and getting a fair price for sustaining a good quality of life. In India, many farmers are committing suicide due to indebtedness which has a direct bearing on the natural calamity as well as fair price after they harvest the products. They are not in a position to repay the bank loan due to low return on investment whereas the same products are bought by the consumers at a high price. Poor farmers also are not aware of the market demands varying from year to year which could be accessed through internet. The needs of the poor must be reviewed and prioritized for intervention through the cooperative society using modern and viable means.

Curriculum and Training

Forming and developing norms of a cooperative society is to be taught to the beneficiary first at the community level who will remain engaged in the organization and management of the cooperative. Systematic training is a pre-condition for managing organizations effectively. Therefore, a curriculum for cooperative registration to begin along with different awareness campaigns of the aspects of compliance to management is to be taught to those who will be engaged for management of cooperative enterprises. The learning contents should incorporate management principles and techniques including human resource management, financial management, marketing management, organizational development, and regular monitoring and evaluation of organizations. This is the point where systematic social audit can be used for effective and efficient functioning. This will go a long way in establishing the road map to social development with the cooperation of the targeted groups making them stakeholders for holistic development.

Mobilization of Resources

The essential requirements for a cooperative organization are members, capital, infrastructure, human resources. The cooperatives are established with the involvement of members and the beneficiaries generating capital from among the members. However, infrastructure and human resources are the basic liabilities as it needs investment of capital. The cooperatives are registered under the Cooperative Society Act which needs a lot of paper work in compliance with the rules and regulations of the Act. Any cooperative to begin with generates fund by selling its share to the members only. Mobilization of capital for the business within the members is a great challenge as no one in this globalised era would like to invest in an uncertain business which may not give them dividends. But cooperative is basically a people's organization protecting the interest of the members in their own business or occupation for which there is need to look at the profit aspect of enterprises. Mobilization of members concerning their trade and occupations is to taken for formation of any cooperative. If the farmers are not getting fair price of their products, cooperatives can process and preserve the products for selling the same at higher prices forming farmers' marketing cooperatives.

Formation of Cooperative Society

Since the acts and rules of cooperative are complicated for the people in general that the professional social workers can help in the formation of the cooperatives by identifying their needs and taking up a feasibility study before formation. Tagore in his experiments in rural reconstruction had stressed upon the formation of such cooperatives based on the needs of the common people including the poor who may not be able to operate singly but can be a member with limited investment in their own interest. Applying the principles of ownership, a cooperative can be beneficiaries' property to alleviate poverty and exploitation by the powerful making profit from the poor. Initially, it may seem a hard and difficult task but training and education of the beneficiary will empower them to perform the responsibility as a member of the organization. Therefore, sensitizing, knowledge building and setting the mindset for development are first and foremost tasks for formation of cooperative organizations.

Operation and Management of Cooperatives

Management of cooperatives is further complicated and are mostly mismanaged due to communication gap between the management and members. The Governing Body and the Executive Body must consist of persons who are knowledgeable about organizations and its management. If not, they have to be first trained in the management of business organizations with basic knowledge, skills and attitude for compliance and applications in the management of the enterprises. As cooperative is a democratic organization with governance of all the members, need to have basic knowledge of the organization and maintenance of the cooperative principles along with compliance to basic duties and rights of a member. Application of strategic management policies would be of great help in managing the cooperatives as the market is open and operates with both opportunities and threats from rival business organizations.

Monitoring and Evaluation

Development of monitoring indicators is essential which works as the watchdog for the growth and fall of the business being carried on. Monthly, quarterly, half yearly and annual monitoring of the activities against the target set is the best policy. Setting achievable targets for sustaining the business is the key to success of a business. As the cooperatives are planned, organized and maintained by the poor, for the poor who may not have the required knowledge and skills to monitor or evaluate the progress of work, it is better to place competent paid staff to monitor and evaluate at the end of each year. Mid-term monitoring and evaluation will provide an opportunity to fill up the gaps, if any, against the set goal. Social work professionals, having knowledge and skill in mobilizing people and resources for monitoring can play a significant role in managing such cooperatives aiming at poverty alleviation through empowerment and sustainable business of the poor and vulnerable population, preventing exploitation by the corporate. Monitoring and evaluation can be done using the modern softwares which can provide information on trends of growth and progress eliminating the long-term cost of manual monitoring and evaluation.

Measuring Growth and Development

Measurement of progress of work in modern times is not a big issue as technology can facilitate a continuous measurement by day, week, month and year at the finger tips. However, qualitative assessment of growth and development is the need of the hour. This can be done by using internal as well as external resources. Failing to measure the growth consciously and continually may endanger the prospects of any business. Operation research for the products and services being rendered by the cooperatives is also a pre-condition to successful business. In keeping with the needs for cooperatives of rural community, especially farmers related to agri-business and allied occupations; businesses are to be planned according to the demands of the market and marketability of the end products which must reach the consumers directly or indirectly. This will enhance the sustainability of growth and development of the cooperative.

Relevance of Tagore's Cooperative Principles to Principles of Social Work

Tagore had shown the way for organizing cooperatives of varied kind with laid down principles to sustain the business of the vulnerable people at the community level. The principles of social work emerged for applications in different methods of social work almost simultaneously in the 1920s and 1930s. It is pertinent to review the principles of group and community organizations of social work with reference to Tagore's principles of cooperative societies for rural and urban communities.

- Principles of community need assessment was advocated by Tagore in the early 20th century while organizing cooperative credit society in 1905 with the farming communities for savings and credits of farmers. Accordingly, the credit cooperative societies were organized in different communities spread across the then undivided Bengal as per the needs of the farmers. These societies organized a number of other services as needed by the farmers from time to time. Social work in the contemporary situation applies the same principles with the added advantage of advanced methodology i.e. identifying the needs and prioritizing the same depending on the urgency of the concerned issues. Basically, it does not differ from Tagore's principles of need based services for the poor. For example, while beginning rural reconstruction in a community, he organized a study of the village to identify the actual needs of the people and decide on the course of action.

- Principles of resource mobilization from and within the community were advocated by Tagore from the beginning of his experiments in rural reconstruction. Social work also believes in the same principles of generating resources from and within which has long lasting effect on the people and the organization making it sustainable. Being dependent on external resources is not the right strategy as it may disrupt the process and services when in crisis. Resource identification and mobilization from and within or at the nearest location is the first step of community organization in social work practice.
- Principles of participation and involvement of the beneficiary was stressed upon by Tagore while organizing the cooperative societies making them members with small contributions so that they take the organization as their own. Social work also stresses on participation and involvement in all the activities of the organization of the people by the people having ownership as stakeholders of their own development. Participation in the development and maintenance of organizations with physical and emotional attachment is the key to success of cooperative societies and is accepted both in social work and Tagore's experiment in rural reconstruction.
- The principles of democratic self-determination was the core policy in Tagore's efforts in organizing cooperatives as he believed that imposing anything from outside for the benefit of the people is harmful as it will make them dependant on external aid and services. Therefore, he applied the policy of developing inbuilt mechanisms based on self-help. Social work also believes in democratic self-determination in application of all its methods of rendering and organizing services for the needy, be it individual, groups or communities. Since

cooperatives are people's organization, they have to decide all the matters related to the business activities, growth and expansion of the organization. All decisions of the cooperatives are taken by the majority following democratic principles.

- Principles of monitoring and evaluation were applied in all the cooperatives organized at community level by the apex cooperative developed for monitoring and evaluating the functioning of the cooperative societies. Social work professionals apply the same principles of monitoring and evaluation of the groups and organizations developed with specific objectives and redesign the strategies, if needed, for achievement of the goals of the organizations. Quarterly and half yearly audit of cooperative societies can be termed as monitoring and annual audit as evaluation of the performance of the people and organizations.
- Principles of social justice form the core values that govern cooperatives organized under his experiments in rural reconstruction. The benefits of cooperative organizations were enjoyed equally by all the members as well as non-members living in harmony. Sharing the benefits is the joy of life resulting in social satisfaction of living together. In social work practice too, the principles of social justice form the core values of the profession. Therefore, correlations between the cooperative principles applied by Tagore and principles of social work do not differ in the true sense. The applications, however, in different contexts, differ in their practice.

Rights-based Approach in Social Work

One of the core values and pillars of social work is human rights. Human rights and social justice are the two sides of the same coin. Tagore's approach to human development was based on the rights of the people to organize them for their common benefit. All kinds of cooperatives discussed in this chapter were meant for socio-economic and cultural development based on social justice which the people in society were deprived of in those days. Rather, they were subject to exploitation by the landlords and merchants. Being a landlord himself, concern for the people, alleviation of poverty, illiteracy and ill health were his prime focus areas. According to The Universal Declaration of Human Rights, "The cooperative society examines the premise that humans are at the threshold of such momentous historical change, making possible the realization of our most broadly and deeply held social values." (United Nations, 1948)[17] As per the observations of Tagore the common people had no faith in claiming or improving their conditions of life. They believed that the conditions of their life is due to their fate gifted from God and they must suffer. Tagore in his experiments in rural reconstructions strived to inculcate faith among the people so they can improve their quality of life as well as claim their rights as human beings by organizing themselves.

Cooperatives and Strength Based Approaches in Social Work

Review of Tagore's experiment in rural reconstruction reveals that in every action he stressed the strength of the people as individuals, groups and communities and channelized the same for self-reliance and sustainable development. Cooperative movement is the most illuminating example of strength based approach for social development. Interestingly, what Tagore could foresee in collective action for social good is by organizing them with the spirit of service for self development and applying their potentialities through organizations founded on their own strength. He believed that providing help and assistance will harm them more than a temporary benefit. Mobilization of internal resources through cooperatives can be sustained as members are the stakeholders of the programme and organization are directed towards benefits for those who are vulnerable in all senses. Strength based approaches emerged in social work literature in the 1970s were practiced in a different form by Tagore in the early 20th century. Therefore, it is justified to say that the varied types of cooperatives organized and managed by the people in communities are the most appropriate strength based approaches to social development.

Conclusion

Cooperative Societies occupy a major space in Tagore's philosophy and approach to social development as applied in varied fields of human life of contemporary society. His observations on the cooperative movement in Sweden and Russia had influenced him to develop cooperatives in India considering the social and economic conditions of the rural masses. He believed that these poor and vulnerable can improve their socio-economic and cultural conditions by forming cooperatives of their own. His far sighted vision was that if these organizations are managed and maintained by the people themselves it can be sustained as long as people need. Today, when we talk of empowerment of the powerless, access to credit and developing skills and competencies of the suffering people, Tagore's approaches and principles remind us the same kind of work done a century ago. The cooperative societies are the example of uniting and empowering the poor for sustainable development. Government's efforts in social welfare and development of the backward people through projects and schemes are failing to achieve their goals since independence mainly because the ownership of the intervention lies with the government and not with the people. Should it have been people oriented projects and schemes like cooperatives of varied nature with ownership of the beneficiary, the situation would have been different than that of the abortive attempts by spending huge sums in the last seven decades. The cooperatives are the organizations of the people and for the people but when taken by the government, it is not of the people but for the people. Recently Birbhum Central Cooperative Bank owned partly by government in the command area has been facing liquidation problem. It does not mean that people's cooperative won't face similar situations. The competitive market today is a challenge to management of cooperatives whether it belongs to the government or the private sector. The financial stability and scientific management are two important components of any business organization. The market a century ago was totally different than what it is today. Rural enterprises now are entering into competition with the enterprises belonging to national and multi-national corporate, hence the plan of action of rural enterprises are to be at par with international business strategies and standards. In global village, we will have to establish global cooperatives for the modern inhabitants with updated knowledge and skills to manage and maintain for sustained growth and development of the members and the organization. It is further interesting to note that what Tagore had envisaged a century back is still relevant and appropriate to modern society. His principles of rural reconstruction were; we shall not develop the villages, but we must ensure that development takes place with the efforts of the villagers. He also believed that there was a need for training and education before organizing people in communities for a sustainable approach to development. He was convinced that only professional expertise can help in furthering the development of people and their organizations. Training and education is essential before going to serve was the feeling and practice of Tagore. Social work education and training meets the need for service which is now professionally accepted and established across the globe. Worthwhile to mention that the term social work was not found in his writings but all the methods, principles, and steps followed by him in his experiments in rural reconstruction are akin to social work as a profession we practice today. Further, social work profession can take his cooperative model and social entrepreneurship for promoting rural community in line with this to deal with issues of poverty, illiteracy, ill health and meeting other social and economic needs of the people and society at large. Cooperatives can be the right organizations for the uplift of the poor and vulnerable communities in our country. Social work professional can take up this as one of the macro practices as community development and make some model cooperatives and villages for others to replicate.

BIBLIOGRAPHICAL REFERENCES

Tagore, Rabindranath; *Gitanjali*, 1910, Visva-Bharati.

Tagore, Rabindranath. *Religion of Man*. Appendix II. p. 126, Visva-Bharati, 2008 (1931).

https://www.google.com/search?q=amul+history+in+brief&rlz=1C1CHBD_enIN816IN816&oq=amul&aqs=chrome.1.69i57j69i59j0l4.6193j0j7&sourceid=chrome&ie=UTF-8

Tagore, Rabindranath; *Cooperative Principles*, 1929, Visva-Bharati.

https://www.ica.coop/en/what-co-operative-0

Tagore, Rabindranath; *Cooperative Principles*, 1929, Visva-Bharati. https://www.ica.coop/en/what-co-operative-0

http://www.sewa.org/About_Us.asp

Address to *Brati Balak Sakha*, 12 April, 1924, Santiniketan. Cited in *Rabindranather Pallipunargathan Prayas*, Dikshit Sinha, p. 221, Paschimbanga Bangla Academi, 2010.

Sinha, Dikshit; *Cooperatives as Tool for Development: Rabindranath Tagore and Organisation of Cooperatives in Early Twentieth Century Bengal, Rabindranath Tagore on Economy, Politics and Society–Contemporary Discourses*. p. 30, Ed. Sebak Jana, Dey Book Concern, Kolkata, 2017.

Ibid., 302.

Malley L.S.O., Birbhum, *Bengal District Gazetteer*, Calcutta, Reprint 1998 (1911). Cited in *Rabindranather Palli Punarghatan Prayas,* Dikshit Sinha, Paschimbanga Bangla Academi, pp. 316-317, 2010.

Tagore, Rabindranath. "Samabaya Malaria Nibaran", 1924, *Rabindra Rachanabali*, p. 569, Visva-Bharati, 1974.

Sinha, Dikshit; *Rabindranather Palli Punargathan Prayas,* Paschimbanga Bangla Academi, pp. 332-333, 2010.

Cited in Sinha, Dikshit; *Cooperatives as Tool for Development: Rabindranath Tagore and Organisation of Cooperatives in Early Twentieth Century Bengal, Rabindranath Tagore on Economy, Politics and Society–Contemporary Discourses*. p. 45, Ed. Sebak Jana, Dey Book Concern, Kolkata, 2017.

UN Declaration of Human Rights, 1948. UNO.

NOTES

1. Tagore, Rabindranath; *Gitanjali*, 1910, Visva-Bharati.
2. Tagore, Rabindranath. *Religion of Man*. Appendix II. pp. 126, 1931, (2008) Visva-Bharati.
3. https://www.google.com/search?q=amul+history+in+brief&rlz=1C1CHBD_enIN816IN816&oq=amul&aqs=chrome.1.69i57j69i59j0l4.6193j0j7&sourceid=chrome&ie=UTF-8

4. *Cooperative Principles*, Rabindranath Tagore, 1929, p. 36, Visva-Bharati.
5. *Ibid*., p. 37.
6. *Ibid*., p. 38.
7. https://www.ica.coop/en/what-co-operative-0
8. Amar Kutir Society has evolved as a self-sufficient organization over the years applying the principle of Tagore, Rural Otganisation for Rural Development.
9. http://www.sewa.org/About_Us.asp
10. Address to *Brati Balak Sakha*, 12 April, 1924, Santiniketan. Cited in *Rabindranather Pallipunargathan Prayas*, Dikshit Sinha, p. 221, Paschimbanga Bangla Academi, 2010.
11. Sinha, Dikshit; *Cooperatives as Tool for Development: Rabindranath Tagore and Organisation of Cooperatives in Early Twentieth Century Bengal, Rabindranath Tagore on Economy, Politics and Society–Contemporary Discourses*. p. 30, Ed. Sebak Jana, Dey Book Concern, Kolkata, 2017.
12. *Ibid*., p. 302.
13. Malley L.S.O., Birbhum, Bengal District Gazetteer, Calcutta, Reprint 1998 (1911). Cited in *Rabindranather Palli Punarghataner Prayas,* Dikshit Sinha, Paschimbanga Bangla Academi, pp. 316-317, 2010.
14. Rabindranath Tagore, "Samabaya Malaria Nibaran", 1924, *Rabindra Rachanabali*, p. 569, Visva-Bharati, 1974.
15. *Rabindranather Palli Punarghatan Prayas,* Dikshit Sinha, Paschimbanga Bangla Academi, pp. 332-333, 2010.
16. Cited in Sinha, Dikshit; *Cooperatives as Tool for Development: Rabindranath Tagore and Organisation of Cooperatives in Early Twentieth Century Bengal, Rabindranath Tagore on Economy, Politics and Society: Contemporary Discourses*. p. 45, Ed. Sebak Jana, Dey Book Concern, Kolkata, 2017.
17. UN Declaration of Human Rights, 1948. UNO.

Afterword

Sesh nahi jaar, sesh katha ke bolbe...(*Gitabitan*, 2012, p. 238).

Who shall sing the songs of one who is endless...
If at first like a blow, in time it will glow
Once clouds have clustered, rain starts to pour
Its water turned ice a river starts to flow
What looks like the end is only superficially so!
Traversing the dark, light appears at the door
The worn out heart breaks, only to revive on its own...
(*Translated by Fakrul Alam, 2018*)

In writing this book we have literally been on an inspiring journey of discovery and insight affirming that very little is impossible if we apply our minds and heart; as has been time and again demonstrated by those innovative thinkers and doers all-over the world reiterating their faith in human potential. Human potential is not bound by lines of geography or nationhood; it is for us to rediscover their innate universality and their sensitivity to human and related conditions. This journey has been that in many ways. The Western mind is now more interested to dig into the *raison d'être* and actions of a poet-philosopher-doer going beyond the universal image of benevolence of the one whose words brought solace to the despondency of Europe preparing for the impending wars. Gandhi called him the Great Sentinel, the conscience of the nation.[1] Tagore's Nobel Prize winning collection of poems, *Gitanjali* (1913) had been cited as a universal message of fortitude, solace and wisdom to the people in troubled times.[2]

Tagore had long rejected the idea of nationalism and had embraced the idea of the universal man; he believed that human problems are interlinked and that their solutions too are to be worked out in cooperation and fellow-feeling. This has been brought out very clearly in Chapter 2. Tagore thought about international humanism very seriously and he believed it to be important in his understanding of education. Of his Visva-Bharati Tagore said, "I have formed the nucleus of an international university as one of the best means of promoting mutual understanding between the East and the West."[3]

About Tagore's ideas of Internationalism, Sten Konow wrote, "It is a poet's vision, but it came at a time when men were in sore need. The gospel of Jesus had proved powerless when people rose against people and each of them in the name of the King of Peace called upon men to take up arms…the outlook in the west seemed hopeless, when the Poet came and asked us to seek salvation through faith in new ideas, wise men of the world smiled but there were individuals who felt that there was yet hope for humanity."[4] For many years Tagore was held in awe, not only as one of the movers of early 20th Century liberal thinking but also for being seen a prophet of peace that vaned with time and changed priorities.[5]

However, the modern Indian response to Tagore is no less significant; we are gradually gaining in historical mileage of putting Tagore in perspective[6] and we are keen to take steps so that we are able to shift from a blind following or imitation to calibrating and testing his ideas and actions and in the process, transforming them to become viable in the changed contemporary times. This can be seen as a major step towards modernity as well as being more in sync with what Tagore believed all his life. There is no advantage to be gained by faithfully keeping the shell of his ideas notionally alive through customs and rituals of which there is great danger of leading to a passivity of spirit. We are gradually realizing the need to put to practice the sustainable ideas that Tagore himself tried (albeit in small sectors) keeping in perspective today's situation and needs. Our awe and admiration has to go through a process of transformation so that we do not merely imitate Tagore but learn to use our own innovative skills and knowledge to fine tune his plans and objectives in order to create a more self-confident human resource free of social ills.

This realization is a product of the many years that the Indian authors have spent in teaching and transmitting the ideas of Tagore to generation of students; their involvement with the neighbouring villages and village societies; and facing the reality of the (in)adequate success of the projects and plans undertaken by the machinery of the State for the uplift of rural life over the years. Quite a many of the plans and programmes have been/are 'protectionist' in nature; they do not have scope for the common person to exercise her agency or make individual effort. The State has not been able to directly touch individual lives or even individual village societies and nor can the State be confident of the trust and faith of the villagers; albeit with variations given the vast number of villages and their conditions. These issues have been dealt with in Chapters 3 and 4.

In the work of rural reconstruction, Tagore created through the various programmes of uplift, a level playing field so that the 'illiterate' and the 'educated' could enter into meaningful dialogue mutually addressing problems and situations. Through this exchange on a level-playing field, the villagers were enabled to exercise their own agency[7] in order to negotiate advantageously with the demands and pace of a changing world and thus overcoming the disadvantages of their circumstances. This dialogue fostered the confidence of the common people and also maintained their dignity upholding their rights as human beings. This has been variously highlighted in the chapters of this book.

Santiniketan and Sriniketan have been places that has always attracted many scholars, academicians, artists, musicians, practitioners and wanderers. In recent times, with the revival of Tagorean ideas and thoughts through translation of his works in many languages, academicians and scholars from various countries are increasingly showing genuine interest in learning about him. The Swiss author is the force behind this volume and it was her idea of such a book for making Tagore accessible to her own students of Social Work in Switzerland, a proposal that the Department of Social Work, Visva-Bharati, Sriniketan gladly and willingly took up. In a way this has been a full cycle starting with Tagore's interactions with Romain Rolland and his complete support to the work of Paul Geheeb post-World War I in Switzerland. This has helped us immensely to wake out of the torpor of 'what else can there be to know' and to ask ourselves the questions, 'Have we explored the possibilities of Tagore's ideas in contemporary times and Are we happy to be in the state of inertia of continuing the legacy through ritualistic obeisance'? This book endeavours to evoke response to the question, 'What could be the contemporary interest areas in the theory and practice of Social Work in the context of Tagore's work and ideas'.

This book is the conjoined effort of European and Indian perceptions of Tagore's contribution in the domain of social mechanisms and social change that are induced and engendered through persistent and persevering efforts to light the sparks within people who generally are unaware of their role in nation building, to become self-igniting flames on the merit of rejuvenated reserves of their human strength. Going through the vast array of Tagore's oeuvre and the presentations in this volume it is clear that Tagore's was one of the earliest cogent voices raised for social work based on the strengths perspective. From the way the Sriniketan Experiment was designed and executed, it is also clear that Tagore had the beginnings of what we now term as 'evidence-based practice'. This book also makes a pitch for human ingenuity and the power of collective activity, the core areas of Tagore praxis. Positing the work of Tagore in his experiment in Rural Reconstruction against the backdrop of the ecological perspective, a few pin-pointed observations can be conclusively inferred–Tagore considered the individual to be the principal agent in terms of creativity and ingenuity; the community within which the individual lives provides the driving force for the individual to take control along with fellowship with others; the cultural and social resources can only be thought of as resources when there is collective participation and engagement while the ultimate measure of human development lies in fulfilling the objectives of humanity sans religion, caste or creed. In the parlance of modern practices of Social Work, it is possible (through a parallel analysis) to identify the micro, meso, exo and macro aspects within which human beings function in Tagorean thought. Tagore's work provides evidence of the interrelationships between the systems impacting on the individual and how the transactions with the systems can be made meaningful in achieving the 'all-round' development of individuals.[8]

The introductory chapter of the volume is followed by a chapter in which we find a socio-historical account of Tagore and his life and the gradual emergence of the thrust areas of his work with people and communities. The chapter discusses at length the plurality and internationalism of Tagore that contributed to his global charisma; it also provides the narrative describing Tagore's rejection of the idea of nationalism. Tagore's ideas if anything, were eclectic and freely absorbed the ideas of many thinkers and doers. Tagore did not affiliate himself with any particular school or schools of thought and it was this that gave him the freedom to strike out on his own. His fundamentals were very clear–his deep faith in the creative spirit of man in fellowship with man.

The subsequent chapters give us accounts of the different kind of activities conducted in Sriniketan, both academic and application of the academic sensibility and understanding for extension activities in the neighbouring villages and communities… The authors have taken care to provide historical information and perspective of the plans, programmes and objectives. A little-known account of Tagore's ideas and practice of cooperatives (Chapter 4) tells us how innovative Tagore was. The authors have worked very closely together so that the individual chapters as far as possible dovetail into each other seamlessly. This was a conscious decision taken at the very outset of the project.

Tagore defies definition; any discussion of his ideas being slotted in one philosophical school of thought or another does not really take us far and we may fail to answer the question, "Can we interpret his ideas on the basis of a well-defined philosophical system of thought?" In his own words, we are able to get clues to his thinking; "It is appropriate to view in a historical way the evolution of the writings of a man who has been writing for a long time....It needs to be taken into account that a set of political ideas did not emerge from my mind at a particular time—they developed in response to life experience and evolved over the years" (Tagore 1929, pp. 337-338). As the political and economic plane shifted and changed so did his own ideas and practices not always following a logical evolutionary process. His core belief in man's capacities was the lodestar around which he arranged and rearranged his Sriniketan Experiment of Rural Reconstruction–he did not waver in this mission but tried to invent and re-invent himself again and again.

In verity, when dealing with the variety and range of Tagore's thoughts, actions and initiatives, it is very difficult to come to clearly formed conclusions–there will always be a sense of something left by the wayside or not adequately highlighted; this holds true for every one of those who inspire us to believe in the ever-renewable creative energies of man. This very focussed volume speaks about that aspect of Tagore or the aspect of his work that does not have the romance of literature and in fact an aspect that has been overshadowed by the poetry that endlessly flowed from him. His literature and poetry too reflect Tagore's deep concern for humanity and for man to stand by man. However, Tagore does not present reality as emphatic and engulfing, that in itself is conceding failure; rather, he laid greater stress on the will to find solutions that will gradually cater to increasing numbers. Tagore's literature, theatre, music and poetry have not been able to maintain intellectual distance from these truths.[9]

The second chapter highlights the issues and situations that we are increasingly facing with an alarming rapidity in the Western countries and spreading to the other parts of the world that are directly impacting individual lives and well-being. Meaningful intervention has to be founded on the precepts of participation, inclusion and the empowerment of autonomy of individuals and collectives. The view proposed in post-modern understanding of Social Work, both theory and praxis, is pluralistic reading where Tagore's thoughts and ideas can be supportive. The underlying spirit of his thoughts helps us in going beyond the beaten track and restoring strength and beauty to what connects rather than what differentiates.

Education for Tagore informed all the other ideas and concepts he engaged with–ideas of nationalism, internationalism, truth, beauty, nature, creativity and rural reconstruction, to mention some of them. Education encompassed all these concepts and more and one can discern in the gestalt a pattern in which all these strands are interwoven. In Tagore's words, "I was brought up in an atmosphere of aspiration, aspiration for the expansion of the human spirit. Such an opportunity has given me confidence in the power of education which is one with life and only which can give us real freedom, the highest that is claimed for man, his freedom of moral communion in the human world" (Tagore: 1929).

The quotation from Saint-Hilaire (2002), a contemporary thinker and follower of Sri Aurobindo (another very important maker of modern India and firm believer in international humanism) makes an interesting point. He says, "The aim of education is always twofold: there is a collective aspect and there is an individual aspect. The individual can have two kinds of relationship with education–one is parasitic in which one uses knowledge as a means of personal growth and the other is symbiotic in which the individual sheds the light of his knowledge on others around him so that they are also brought into the light."[10] Tagore many years earlier was always concerned with the symbiotic aspect of education when he urged that it was the responsibility of every educated individual to extend himself or herself so that the not so fortunate could also be included in the halo of knowledge. Tagore justifies his stand, "One principle in human life is sociability. Man finds his true shelter in society through contact. When man's relationship finds expansion in his surroundings, in his home and outside, the largeness of that relationship in itself pleases him. Our deep satisfaction lies in a relationship which is not based on any selfish consideration of utility, advantage or business, but on the bonds of kinship which transcends all self-centred interests" (Tagore: 1930).

The final word:

This chapter started with a Tagore song that talks about the infinite nature of cosmic life embracing the world and its inhabitants in one circle that passes from dark to light; from clouds to purifying rain and our hurts transformed into the fruits of our life. This embodies Tagore's striving towards that bigger picture; the distant future and in attaining the fruits of life. This was the distinct trademark of Tagorean thoughts, never the narrow sectarian goals but the call of wide open world to humanity. There is greater need to turn to this core idea of Tagore.

In the act of remembering great minds, thinkers and educators, we assume the 'burden' of establishing that particular person's 'relevance', 'appropriateness' or 'value' in the context of his/her times *vis-à-vis* encountering the problems or conditions of modernity. Every life comes and goes but not every life gives a special touch to the human story; we try to make those moments important; the ways in which our thoughts have been influenced and our own sensibilities carved. This aggregation of human effort and striving is very crucial to human history; as is the belief in the continuity of life and humanity.

Often, Tagore is seen in the context of his times, while in reality he had set his sights on a distant future when the colonial power would leave India and the county would be thrown upon its own resources for all the services and functions. His work was to prepare man to be ready to take the challenge and face up to the task.

Jokhon Porhbe Na Mor Payer Chinho…
(*Gitabitan,* 2012, p. 548).

When my footsteps no longer leave their mark on this road
When I no longer dock my boat in this waterfront
When I've wrapped up all transactions
Met all debts, settled all accounts,
And stopped coming to this fair,
How will it matter if you fail to remember me then
Or don't call out my name while gazing at the stars?

When the strings of my tanpura gather dust
When, ah, weeds creep up all house doors
When even the garden has put on the garbs of the wild
When moss has covered the pond's banks on all sides
How will it matter if you fail to remember me then
    Or don't call out my name while gazing at the stars?

Then banks will resound with the flute's tunes as they do now
    Time will flow on smoothly as ever
    Time will flow on, ah, as time does forever
        Boats will swarm docks then as they do now
        Cowherds will play on as cows graze in this field
        How will it matter if you fail to remember me then
            Or don't call out my name while gazing at the stars?

    Who will then say I was not there at that dawn?
        All games will go on and, ah, I will be in them all
        You'll call me anew and bind me with ever new ties
            I'll keep coming and going but remain the same me
        How will it matter if you fail to remember me then
            Or don't call out my name while gazing at the stars?

(*Translated by Fakrul Alam, 2018*).

BIBLIOGRAPHICAL REFERENCES

Bhattacharya, Sabyasachi, *The Defining Moments in Bengal (1920-1947)*, 2014, New Delhi, Oxford University Press, pp. 1-45.

Dutta, Krishna and Andrew Robinson, *Selected Letters of Rabindranath Tagore*, 19917, p. xxiv.

Ecological Approach http://ecologicaltheory.tripod.com/ accessed 03.05.2019

Gandhi, M.K., in his essay, "A Great Sentinel", *Young India*, 13 October, 1921.

Kabir, Humayun (ed.) *Poems of Rabindranath Tagore*, Calcutta, UBSPD and Visva-Bharati, 2005.

Kaempchen, Martin and Imre Bangha (eds.), *Rabindranath Tagore: One Hundred Years of Global Reception*, Orient Blackswan, 2014, pp. ix-xxiii.

Konow Sten, "Visva-Bharati and its Ideals" in *Modern Review*, February,1925.

Lago, Mary (ed.) *Imperfect Encounter: Letters of William Rothenstein and Rabindranath Tagore 1911-1941*, 1972.

Saint Hilaire, P.B., *Education and the aim of Human Life*. Pondicherry, Sri Aurobindo Ashram, 2002.
Tagore, Rabindranath, "An Eastern University", *English Writings of Rabindranath Tagore (EWRT),* Volume 2, New Delhi, Sahitya Akademi.
Gitabitan, Kolkata, Visva-Bharati, 2012.

NOTES

1. M.K. Gandhi, in his essay, "A Great Sentinel", *Young India*, 13 October, 1921.
2. Mary Lago (ed.) *Imperfect Encounter: Letters of William Rothenstein and Rabindranath Tagore 1911-1941*, 1972.
3. Tagore, "An Eastern University", *EWRT,* Volume 2, see also, Amartya Sen, quoted in Krishna Dutta and Andrew Robinson (eds.) *Selected Letters of Rabindranath Tagore*, 19917, p. xxiv.
4. Sten Konow, "Visva-Bharati and its Ideals" in *Modern Review*, February 1925.
5. Martin Kaempchen and Imre Bangha (eds.), *Rabindranath Tagore: One Hundred Years of Global Reception*, Orient Blackswan, 2014, pp. ix-xxiii.
6. Sabyasachi Bhattacharya, *The Defining Moments in Bengal (1920-1947)*, 2014, New Delhi, Oxford University Press, pp. 1-45.
7. Tagore did not use the word 'agency'; he chose the word 'atmashakti' which loosely translated means self-confidence and self-possession.
8. See http://ecologicaltheory.tripod.com/ accessed 03.05.2019.
9. See Rabindranath Tagore's poem, (extract) "I live in a small corner in the perpetual exile of prestige, seated by a narrow window on society's high platform/Sometimes I have ventured near their homes but have lacked the courage to enter/ Come, poet of mute obscure men, give voice to their hidden sorrow, fill with life and joy this dry songless land, release the spring in its heart" (translated by Humayun Kabir). 'Poet of Man' in Humayun Kabir (ed.) *Poems of Rabindranath Tagore*, 2000, Visva-Bharati and UBSPD, p. 240.
10. P.B. Saint Hilaire, *Education and the aim of Human Life*. Pondicherry, Sri Aurobindo Ashram, 2002.

Index